Praise for *Messy Hope*

Messy Hope is the kind of book I wish I had had in the early days of private practice. The hope busters, hope builders, and hopeful truths offer a place to evaluate our own response and learn a better way to support those crushed by the painful reality of anxiety, depression, and suicidal thoughts. —Dr. Michelle L. Bengtson, clinical neuropsychologist and author, *Hope Prevails* and *Breaking Anxiety's Grip*

Lori does a magnificent job of weaving relevant and enjoyable stories with compelling truths so you won't be overwhelmed. Instead, you'll be encouraged and empowered. —Dr. Kathy Koch, founder of Celebrate Kids, Inc., and author, *Screens and Teens, 8 Great Smarts, Start with the Heart*, and *Five to Thrive*

One hundred percent of parents have struggling kids. That's why *Messy Hope* is such an important read. In its pages, find relatable stories of parents and kids who grapple with deep issues, Scriptural encouragement as you navigate a new normal, and practical steps to take in the aftermath of stress. —Mary DeMuth, author, *Building the Christian Family You Never Had*

The stories, insights, practical wisdom, and God-confidence in *Messy Hope* will change your life. As a pastor, multiple copies of this encouraging book will always be available in my office. I will use it as a powerful source of hope for those who struggle. —Kurt W. Bubna, pastor and author

Feelings of helplessness and hopelessness are not unique to children; parents feel these same emotions when helping their kids navigate messy realities like depression, anxiety, fear, and worry. This book equips parents for the journey with practical and faith-filled advice. —Michael Tiede, MA, LP, dad, adolescent and child psychologist
  —Vicki Tiede, MEd, MMin, mom, speaker, Bible teacher, and author, *When Your Husband Is Addicted to Pornography: Healing Your Wounded Heart*

Lori lays out a remarkably clear-eyed and encouraging path for how to support a hurting child back to strength and godly health. Confused or desperate parents will finish this book with an abundance of what all parents need most—Christ's gracious hope. —Patricia Raybon, author, *I Told the Mountain to Move: Learning to Pray So Things Change*

In *Messy Hope* you will discover that God's vision and purpose for your kids is not a life without struggle but rather a life walking with Him in and through every high and every low, no matter how deep those lows may be. —Dr. Rob Rienow, cofounder, Visionary Family Ministries

As a mother, I've dealt with it all: anxiety, depression, and suicidal ideation. It's been a lonely journey . . . until now. Thank you, Lori, for helping us know we're not alone and giving us much needed wisdom to lead our kids well when life is hard. —Jill Savage, author, *No More Perfect Kids*, and host, *No More Perfect* podcast

i

Messy Hope

Our children are facing the greatest mental health crisis the world has ever known. What we need in this season is help and hope. Like a trusted friend and seasoned mentor, Lori gently walks alongside parents who are weary and maybe a little afraid pointing to the source of all hope—Jesus. —Lee Nienhuis, speaker and author of *Brave Moms, Brave Kids* and *Countercultural Parenting*

Messy Hope offers struggling parents a bear hug to sustain their souls. We all need Wildenberg's heartfelt insights and empathetic tools to support the children around us through this generation's growing issues with depression and anxiety. —Tina Yeager, LMHC, life coach, speaker, host *Flourish-Meant* podcast; author, *Beautiful Warrior*

I am always looking for wise, trustworthy, and life-changing books I can confidently give my clients. This is one of those books. " —Sean Taylor, M.S., LMFT, LAC director and co-founder of Cornerstone Christian Counseling

Messy Hope is a book about honesty—getting honest about both the mess of our actual lives and the hope found in God's promises. You will be better equipped to love people by reading this book. —Alexandra Kuykendall, cofounder, The Open Door Sisterhood; author, *Loving My Actual Life*

Messy Hope is a breath of fresh air. As a school counselor and therapist, I see the mental health needs of kids get younger and more complicated each school year. I'm grateful for the wisdom and love Lori shares with parents who need real advice with a compassionate heart. —Brenda L. Yoder, LMHC, speaker, and author, *Fledge: Launching Your Kids Without Losing Your Mind*

Discover within these pages a good dose of spiritual insight and wisdom along with the practical steps needed to help your child and renew hope—for you both! —Kristen Hatton, MA, author, *The Gospel-Centered Life in Exodus for Students*, *Face Time: Your Identity in a Selfie World*, and *Get Your Story Straight*

Parenting a child through anxiety and depression isn't for the faint of heart and can often feel isolating. Lori is a trustworthy guide who comes alongside us offering us hope, wisdom, and practical help. —Sarah Bragg, podcast host and author, *A Mother's Guide to Raising Herself*

Lori does a beautiful job sharing real-life stories that remind the reader that while life is filled with bumps along the way, God's presence can change it all. Thank you for this beautiful offering and reminder that while life is messy, hope is always around every corner! —Maggie John, television anchor and producer, *Context Beyond the Headlines*

Written from a mother's heart, *Messy Hope* is certain to help you build hope for your children. It offers tools and applications to help arm your children with hope too. This book is sure to bring hope to a hopeless world! —Laine Lawson Craft, author, *Enjoy Today Own Tomorrow*

messy
HOPE

Help Your Child Overcome Anxiety, Depression, or Suicidal Ideation

LORI WILDENBERG

NEW HOPE®
PUBLISHERS
Imprint of Iron Stream Media

Birmingham, Alabama

Other Books by Lori Wildenberg

Messy Journey
The Messy Life of Parenting

New Hope Publishers is an imprint of Iron Stream Media
IronStreamMedia.com

Library of Congress Control Number: 2021937464

ISBN: 978-1-56309-478-1 paperback
ISBN: 978-1-56309-479-8 ebook

1 2 3 4 5—25 24 23 22 21
Printed in the United States of America

DEDICATION

This book is dedicated to those who
live in messy hope today
in the anticipation of abiding
in true hope tomorrow.
With hope for a future,

Lori

Simple Faith

Oh give me but a simple faith,
A faith that faileth never.
A faith that's built upon Thy Rock
So strong nothing can sever.

Oh give me but a simple faith,
My anchor in all weather.
No storm can tear me from You,
Simple faith my only tether.

Oh give me but a simple faith,
I need thee every minute.
For there is no place in time
Without Your presence in it.

Oh give me but a simple faith,
To trust and never doubt.
That when my earthly race is run
My simple faith wins out.

Rockman

CONTENTS

ACKNOWLEDGMENTS

There were moments this book was tough to write. My daughter's pain was like shards of glass that pierced my heart. I feared this project would stir up those dark emotions in her, but she encouraged me to press forward. Helping others has been part of the healing process.

So, thank you, Kendra, for openly sharing your journey to help those struggling and those who love the strugglers. We need hope in this hard world. I believe this book with your story illuminates that hope.

With a heart filled with faith, hope, and love, I want to express my gratitude to my husband, Tom. He read every word of the manuscript with a keen eye for detail along with a tender heart. He (bravely) offered invaluable insights and suggestions. I love you and I am blessed to do life with you.

To my ever-growing family: Courtney, Jake, Samantha, and Kendra, plus your spouses Jaime, Alex, and Collin. Your interest, laughter, and prayers carried me through the process. And thanks for allowing me to share parts of your lives as well.

To my faithful and faith-filled friends and family, you have abundantly blessed me, shed tears with me, and prayed for me during the writing of this work: Julianne Adams, Pat Appel, Vicki Brock, Keri Buisman, Becky Clark, Jill Gillis, Paula Gleason, Nina Hinds, Peggy Holland, Katie McElroy, Diane Mueller, Karen Murkowski, Amy Raye, Darcy Robertson, Marianne Schmitt, Stacey Van Horn, and Elsa Wolff. A special thanks to Maureen Behrens, who invested her time, talent, and heart while poring (and sometimes crying) over the manuscript. Thanks for being my cheerleaders. I cherish you all.

To my Moms Together Facebook Mentor Team (Eve Rosno, Julie Sanders, Emily Scott, Dolores Smyth, Elizabeth Spencer, Linda Tang, and Brenda Yoder), thank you for your faithfulness to minister to moms, to each other, and to me during the process of writing this book. You are a blessing.

To my Iron Stream/New Hope family, thank you for your continued support and trust. Ramona Richards, your belief in this message and in me provided the fuel to keep on keeping on. Big thanks to John Herring, Tina Atchenson, Susan Cornell, Kim McCulla, and Bradley Isbell for your part in getting this book published and into the hands of those who desperately need its message. You are the best.

And to my Lord and Savior, Jesus Christ, who plants eternity in our hearts and is the true anchor of hope. To God be the Glory.

INTRODUCTION

Hope Needed

I have told you these things, so that in me you may
have peace. In this world you will have trouble.
But take heart! I have overcome the world.

—John 16:33

Life was too sad, too much, too hard. She was past the point
of tears; she was numb and done. The twenty-three-year-
old college student made her decision. She took the bottle and
gulped down the amount of liquid that would guarantee no
more pain. She laid down, closed her eyes, and waited.

This young woman felt like many other young people feel.
She felt hopeless in a hard world. Depleted hope shows itself
in depression, anxiety, and suicide. The statistics for each of
these tragic experiences are climbing at exponential rates. It
is commonplace to know a young person who struggles with
mental illness or has taken their own life.

Parents, we must act. We cannot stand idly by while the
state of the culture or the tragedy of mental illness rips our
children from us. We cannot accept this as the new normal.
Because we live in a hard world, we must prepare our kids
for struggles and suffering. They need to be armed with hope.
Hope is a weaponized bear hug, a mixture of strength
and tenderness, activated following hurt. It gently whispers, "It
will be OK. Your circumstances are temporary."

Hope embraces us then propels us upward while it fights
despair. No one seeks hardship. We run from pain and
suffering. Pre-coronavirus, we may have expressed, "I just
want my child to be happy." Post-Covid, we realize it is more
realistic to state, "Challenges and discouragement will be a
part of my kid's human experience." Now, more than ever, we

know our children will face difficulty and disappointment. They are human beings who will experience a full life. A life with good, hard, sad, and scary things.

Sadness moved difficulty and disappointment to depression and hopelessness for the twenty-three-year-old. She wrote, "It's been two years, and this isn't going to get better. I cannot live feeling this way anymore."

She goes on to describe the action she took to stop the pain, "One night, during my last semester of college, I researched how much of a certain medication I would have to take for me to not wake up. Of course, not wanting to chance it, I bought an extra bottle 'just in case.'

"The next day I quit my job, told my friends I was going to be leaving school and commuting from home to college. I started packing up my belongings in my room so my parents would not have to deal with it later.

"That night I drank the suggested amount and the 'just in case,' turned off the lights and cried, waiting for the medication to take effect. To my dismay, about 24 hours later, I woke up— with nothing more than some abdominal pain and drowsiness as a reminder of my attempt. I screamed and cried and sunk further into my bed, yelling at God for keeping me in this place I hated so much."

This is a portion of what Kendra wrote in a blog to help others battling depression. She is passionate about being there for those who are experiencing dark times.

So am I. I am Kendra's mom.

Today, many people, many children, feel hopeless. Their brain is unhappy, filled with fear, worry, and self-doubt. "Things will never change. Life will never get better," the hopeless culture screams. For this reason, suicide has become the second leading cause of death in young people (with accidents being the first cause).[1] We see evidence of the lack of hope in mental illness exponentially explode and manifest itself in loneliness, anxiety, depression, fearfulness, and suicide. Statistics from the National Health Service (NHS) show that "12.8 percent— roughly one in eight, five- to 19-year-olds had at least one mental health disorder when assessed in 2017."[2]

"Never in my wildest dreams would I have thought I would say, 'My nine-year-old is on antidepressants.' At five years of age, when her peers were expressing joy, contentment, and able to self-regulate, my daughter wasn't." —Marcy

"This figure rises to 16.9 percent of 17- to 19-year-olds. The analysis also finds that one in four children aged 11 to 16 with a mental health problem have self-harmed or attempted suicide at some point. This figure rises to almost half of young people aged 17 to 18 with a disorder."[3]

Are depression and anxiety the new normal? "Some experts are suggesting that anxiety and depression are so common in our youth, and so understandable, that we should accept them as normal."[4] We cannot accept this. This is not normal.

Hopeless people are hyper-focused on the negative, they fixate on the problem, are overwhelmed with the stresses of life, and may feel like a victim. Life feels out of control.

We talk about training our kids to be resilient, to be able to adapt to life's misfortunes and setbacks. Yet we need more than resiliency to break through the darkness of hopelessness. We need resiliency plus the light and strength of supernatural hope. This is our challenge, moms and dads. We must battle against hopelessness.

Our kids will live life in the unexpected. Hopefully, they may never again go through a time of sheltering in place. But it is certain there is no shelter from fear, frustration, and sadness. Stress, adversity, and perhaps trauma will be part of their life story. Our kids need to gain a different perspective, one that sees past the present struggle and recognizes hope for a future.

Even in hardship, life can be managed. Accepting and anticipating change aids in coping and adapting. Life does not unfold in expected ways.

God wants His people to be hopeful and hope-filled. Meld faith in a great big God with trust in a trustworthy Lord to create hope. True hope is birthed in suffering.

Kendra's reflections are sprinkled through this book. Some of those reflections are excerpts from a blog she wrote. Many other people have courageously and vulnerably shared their stories as well. Many who opened their lives to me, and now to you, chose to have an alias assigned to their name to protect their privacy or their children's. All who shared, told their stories to bless and help someone else. They are my heroes!

In John 16:33, Jesus tells us we will have trouble in this world. Thanks to the pandemic we grasp His meaning. He also tells us to take heart because He has overcome the world. Jesus describes the very thing we need to live on planet earth—hope, a hopeful and hope-filled vision. He wants us to experience peace in Him, not in our stuff or situation.

Do you want to live a hope-filled life in a troubled world? Do you want your kids to take heart and be hopeful? There are ways you and I can facilitate hope growth in our children (and in ourselves) so our lives can be fully lived despite hardship that may come.

One way to facilitate hope growth is to understand the brain. A brain that is in overdrive has difficulty distinguishing physical pain from emotional hurt, separating others' pain from one's own despair, and imagined fears from real ones.[5] This is why realism is more important than positivity.

We must discuss realistic hard things. When we talk about embracing and cultivating hope in our families, it is not about presenting a positive perspective. By examining trouble we might face in life, we are better equipped to deal with hard life moments. We need to examine how we, as parents, deal with difficulty. Once we are equipped to face hardship with the hope that Jesus brings, we can model messy hope to navigate a messy life. Then we are ready to train our kids in ways to strengthen their spiritual hope muscle so they too can step up with hopefulness.

Each chapter contains personal stories, scripture, and cutting-edge information. Every chapter concludes with hope blockers, hope builders, hopeful truths, and a prayer. You will be armed with spiritual and practical weapons of hope to battle life's hardships.

Together we will discover the hope-filled tools the Lord provides and pass them along to our children. When our kids receive hope training, they are more prepared to move forward and look upward.

Join Kendra and me in the fight against hopelessness. We must awaken and strengthen hope in ourselves and in our families. When our kids feel worthy, they are secure and believe their life has purpose, even when life disappoints.

We can empower our kids to receive that *spiritual hope bear hug* and wield the *supernatural weapon of hope* so they can move forward and upward even in, especially in, the hard, unexpected times.

Hopeful Truths

Our children are not immune to difficulty and disappointment. God has given us tools to live in the unexpected. (These tools are described in the upcoming chapters.)

Supernatural hope frees us and propels us upward.

Worthiness, safety, and purpose grow hope.

Prayer

Father, our children desperately need to grasp hold of the hope found in You. This world screams of hopelessness. Silence that message. Please open our children's ears and remove the veil from their eyes so they can see the hope only Jesus can provide. Give us the words and wisdom to help our children embrace true hope based on faith and trust in You, our great and good God. In the powerful name of Jesus, Amen.

Now faith is confidence in what we hope for and assurance about what we do not see.

—Hebrews 11:1

Chapter 1

WHICH WAY?

Then you will know which way to go, since you have never been this way before.

—Joshua 3:4

Do you recall the scene in *The Wizard of Oz* where Dorothy comes to a fork in the road and asks Toto, "Now which way do we go?"

"Pardon me. That way is a very nice way," Scarecrow responds, pointing left.

"Who said that?" Dorothy asks.

"It's pleasant down that way too," an agreeable Scarecrow responds.[6]

A fork in the road presents us with a decision to make. Sometimes the path we choose brings us to a detour. Could it be we might be the cause of the delay? Is there something that needs to be learned on the detour?

When I come across an orange sign that says, "Detour ahead," I feel deflated. No one wants to take a detour. We create a detour for ourselves when we get sidetracked or make a wrong choice. Distractions, self-made detours, take us off the direct way God has for us.

Some describe faith as their true north. Sinful distractions cause our spiritual compass to malfunction. Like the Scarecrow, I have found the best way to go is sometimes hard to discern.

Distraction

Adults and kids alike may take their eyes off the path God has for them. Instead they set their sights on people-pleasing or happiness-chasing. They are tempted to look to the left or to the right, not straight ahead or upward. These distractions make us directionally challenged and lead to wrong choices which inevitability causes suffering.

Impulsivity is a quality that does not consider long-term consequences. I know a young woman who has made some bad choices in her life. Those choices are serious enough to potentially bring a prison sentence.

She has openly shared her struggle with me. We reflect on past poor choices, evaluate present decisions, and assess future actions. Together, we laid out two timelines. One timeline ended in prison, the other in freedom. We talked about which behaviors would bring blessings and which ones would bring bondage.

"With each opportunity presented to you, you have a choice to make. Ask yourself, 'Will this lead to prison or to freedom?'"

After talking we discovered she is driven by the need to be loved by others. She believes people-pleasing could make that happen. She also chases hard after instant gratification, things she believes will bring happiness in the moment.

Some suffering comes about from choices other people make. Another type of pain is the result of living in a fallen world with broken people. And other suffering, like this young adult is experiencing, is the direct result of sinful choices. Both good and bad choices have consequences. Freedom or bondage. Hope or hopelessness. Hope brings freedom.

Delay

Freedom is the fruition of hope. It is the big sigh of an exhaled, "Thank you, Jesus." Have you noticed it never arrives early? God's timing is always perfect. It is exactly on time. Never late and never early. This drives me crazy. Just think of all the peace that could be experienced if God moved before the critical moment.

Standing on the precipice of that critical moment is exactly where my feet must be planted. My level of anticipation for what God might do is high. He has my full attention. Maybe that is the point. We are to look up and seek Him rather than find peace in the removal of our discomfort. I wonder, is ultimate peace complete trust?

Sometimes we are asked to wait even longer than the critical moment. That waiting time is often filled with discouragement and frustration.

May and June were two months where a wedding should have happened. The beach wedding in May fell through due to venue details. Kendra and Collin regrouped and scheduled a mountain wedding in June.

March 19, 2020 the Colorado State Government began to shut down. All nonessential licenses ceased being issued. This included marriage licenses. No one knew how long this would be the case.

Kendra and Collin did not think their marriage license was nonessential. They decided it was wise to secure theirs. They drove to the Jefferson County Courthouse in Golden, Colorado.

"We missed getting our license by one hour!" Disappointment was evident in their voices.

"We will find an office that is open. In the whole state of Colorado there has to be one." Determination quickly replaced disappointment. This couple was on a mission. They reached out to ten counties. All ten where shut down.

The eleventh and last county they contacted was Larimer County, about an hour and thirty-minute drive. There was no answer; with high hopes, they left a voice mail stating their request.

Angela Myers, the clerk and recorder from Larimer County, returned their voice mail the following day.

"My husband and I have been married for over thirty years. Marriage is such a blessing. It is the greatest thing in the world."

Collin keyed into the word *blessing* and thought, "She must have a faith!"

Angela continued, "I suspect the governor's orders will close us today. If you can get up here as soon as possible we should be able to get you in."

Braving a Colorado snowstorm, Kendra and Collin drove two agonizingly slow hours to reach their destination. Relief washed over them. They arrived in time. As they stood in line with other couples, they pondered, "We get our license. Fill it out later. Then what? What if no one is here to process it? It is only good for thirty-five days."

They sat down with the clerk. "You can take the license home and send it back. Or you can sign it and self-solemnize."

Kendra and Collin exchanged a glance and shrugged, "We don't know what the future holds. Let's do this now."

No music, no vows, no family, no friends. Only proof of not being related was required. They got married. Right there in Larimer County with only the clerks and other county customers as witnesses to their marriage.

This action relieved some of the pressure. No longer did they worry, "What if we can't get married?" Yet they still wanted to do the ceremony and celebration. Kendra wanted to have her dad walk her down the aisle. They desired to repeat their vows in front of family and friends. They wanted their marriage mentor to officiate. They hoped to see their wedding plans realized.

The wedding they planned was replaced with the new reality. Social distancing, sheltering in place, safer at home, and numbers of guests were now part of the discussion. The June celebration was moved to the twelfth of July, in the hopes that the wedding they planned would be able to take place.

The new requirements for numbers of people at restaurants and other similar venues were determined partly by square feet. Kendra and Collin needed to rethink their July celebration and their guest list. The bridal party, the groom's family, and the bride's family brought Kendra and Collin's celebration to the location's capacity.

Along with the bride and groom and the groom's parents, we settled on four smaller events with different guests attending different celebrations. A Blessing Party, the Colorado Mountain Wedding-Reception, a Minnesota Lake Party, and a Parents of the Groom Gathering.

Guests needed to be notified of the changes. Kendra and Collin, Collin's parents, Tom and I dreaded telling friends and family they couldn't attend the wedding. We were thankful we had alternative parties planned.

The couple gained hope from the gracious responses of their guests. "We totally understand. This is so hard. We support the decisions you need to make under these circumstances." Tears were shed.

"The hardest part was telling the Nanas they couldn't come. I did not want them traveling on a plane to get here. I know they would have come if I didn't tell them no," Kendra lamented.

Both Nanas encouraged Kendra. They appreciated her concern for their well-being. They generated hope in a hard situation. Their response, along with other grace-filled guests, was understanding and loving.

We can be vessels of hope when others experience delay and disappointment. Hope came in the form of the Larimer clerk, supportive family, and gracious friends who exuded love and compassion with the news of the changes.

We can train our kids to have empathy for another's struggle. When we respond with love and encouragement, God will use us as conduits of hope in a hard situation.

No one would have expected the marriage journey to be filled with so many detours. God stretches us in those detours. Think of Moses who stood before Pharaoh ten times before Pharaoh released the Hebrew slaves (Exodus 6–12). In faith, Joshua led the Israelites to march around Jericho every day for six days and then seven times on the seventh day. On the seventh day and the seventh time circling the city walls, they collapsed (Joshua 6). Naaman was healed of his leprosy after he dipped himself in the Jordan River seven times (2 Kings 5).

God could have provided an immediate quick fix to Moses, Joshua, and Naaham but He didn't. This tells us, God is about the journey, the process. Delays and detours are faith builders. If we fix our eyes on God rather than the detour, faith will grow and hope will bloom.

Dead End

Eventually, a detour gets you to your destination. But a dead end? Now that is a hard stop, a complete about-face.

What if you do not want to turn around and go back the way you came? What if you are between a rock and a hard place? Where is God in the dead end?

Moses was in this very situation when he was leading the Israelites out of Egypt and Pharaoh had a change of heart and chased them down. There they were, the Red Sea in front of them and the Egyptian army bearing down on them. A dead end; a hard stop. Nowhere to go.

God made a way where there was no way. He parted the Red Sea and created a space for the Israelites to move safely through to get to the other side. The ground beneath them was not muddy or wet. It was firm and dry. The Israelites escaped and witnessed the Egyptian army being swept away when the sea returned to its place (Exodus 14:15–31).

The Israelites saw God's great power displayed against the Egyptians. They feared the Lord and put their trust in Him and in Moses.

The Red Sea Way

God parted the Red Sea for Kendra, too. He made a way where there appeared to be no way.

"I promise I will get us down the mountain as fast as I can. I just drove up from Denver and I-70 is a parking lot." The ambulance driver offered determination and optimism.

"I'm not worried. I'm praying." I needed more than human positivity, I needed supernatural intervention.

Kendra was in the back of the ambulance, unconscious. She had been in a snowboard accident in Winter Park, Colorado. She was bleeding internally and needed emergency surgery.

We wound down Berthoud Pass without a problem. The ambulance careened onto I-70.

"I don't get it. There are no cars."

"I get it. I'm praying," I replied from the passenger seat.

Tom was also driving down the mountain; he was about twenty minutes behind the ambulance. His plan was to meet us at the hospital. When he entered the freeway, he was stuck in the typical Saturday post-skiing traffic.

When the ambulance arrived at St. Anthony Hospital, a trauma one center, the staff was waiting for Kendra. Kendra's spleen had ruptured. She had lost a lot of blood. If we had arrived twenty minutes later, she would not have made it.

God parted the Red Sea. He made a way where there was no way. Hope springs forth in the impossible moments.

Disappointment

God is the God of the impossible. In some cases, believers are to sit back, trust, and wait while they watch His glory pass by. Other times He invites His people into the process. Disappointment has the potential to be God's invitation for our participation.

In Exodus 14:15 the Lord said to Moses, "Why are you crying out to me? Tell the Israelites to move on." The escape from Egypt was not easy. This exodus was unfolding in unexpected ways. The Israelites were afraid and ready to turn back.

The Lord wanted the Israelites to move forward. He wanted them to participate in their exit plan, even though they were discouraged and distraught.

My friend Nina told me about an experience a newly graduated high school senior had with disappointment.

As a senior, this student was making college plans. Her counselor recommended she apply to one school; she chose to apply to another. Once she applied to the school of her choice, she was accepted. Covid delayed her ability to visit the school.

After acceptance, she was able to fully checkout the school. She felt discouraged and disappointed. Her post high school life was not looking like she pictured. The school was not what she expected. It was definitely not for her.

She needed prayer and wise counsel. She reached out to Nina. They had a bond. They had been praying together for most of the school year.

"Mrs. Hinds, I don't know what to do. I don't want to attend this school. I won't get into another. It's too late. I want to apply to the school my counselor recommended. I feel embarrassed to tell him this because I didn't follow his advice."

Nina encouraged the young woman to move forward, to push past the embarrassment. She arranged a Zoom meeting for the three of them to come up with a strategy. Knowing Nina would be a part of the conversation helped dissolve some of the discomfort the young woman was experiencing. As God would have it, the counselor had a relationship with the faculty at the school the student was now interested in attending. Not only was he an alum but he had also previously been on staff at the school.

It was May 30th and the applications were due June 1st. The counselor called the school and suggested they consider this student. The young woman did her part and got her financial paperwork together.

She was accepted and she received a scholarship. Nina and the young graduate reflected on the disappointment and then the resolution to that disappointment. Embarrassment could have prevented forward motion. As it turned out, the disappointment led to a God appointment.

Just as the Israelites needed to move on, move forward, so did this student. To claim hope in disappointment or discouragement, sometimes God invites us to join Him in the process. When we participate with Him, resilience is built and confidence strengthened.

God's Way

The path God lays out is not always one I want to join Him on. The verse in Isaiah 55:8–9 reminds me, God's thoughts and ways are not the same as mine.

> "For my thoughts are not your thoughts,
> neither are your ways my ways,"
> declares the Lord.

"As the heavens are higher than the earth,
so are my ways higher than your ways
and my thoughts than your thoughts."

This verse is often quoted during hard times, like when someone has received a devastating diagnosis or experienced a great loss. In those moments, I find myself resisting His way. I prefer He ride shotgun rather than take the wheel.

This was the case for me when I visited with my parents while my dad was in the hospital.

My mom lifted the fork to my dad's mouth. His eyes were filled with love as she fed him. I felt frustrated. *He'll never get better if she keeps babying him*, I thought. I was determined Pops would beat this thing. *All he has to do is put forth a little effort, have a good attitude, and embrace his faith.*

Only a few weeks prior, I sat on my parents' bed to talk with my dad. He was preparing to go to the hospital for some cancer treatments. Pops filled his right pocket with the stuff splayed out on his dresser. As a kid, I watched him do this before he went to work. His wallet, some spare change, and his keys were the items he always included. I found comfort observing this ritual.

This day he grabbed his wallet, dropped it into his right pants pocket, tossed in some change, and picked up his keys only to set them back down on the dresser. The pit in my stomach grew. My dad did not need his keys. Pops was dying. My mom knew it; my dad knew it. I refused to accept it.

It can be hard to deal with reality, to accept the unacceptable. Death is a certainty. My mom understood this as she fed her husband as he lay in his hospital bed.

Pops never did return home. He was right, he did not need his keys. My mom, sister, brother, sister-in-law, and I were with him when he took his final breath. My prayer before he passed was that he would have an abundant heavenly homegoing and that I would have the privilege of seeing him reach for Jesus.

God was gracious. He granted both prayers. I miss my dad and I know death does not have the final say. God's will was done. And mine . . . well, His ways are not mine. Yet, I do have the promise of eternal life. And the promise of eternity is ultimate hope.

A New Direction

When life unfolds in an unexpected or unwanted way, a new path needs to be created. The dreams our kids have may be realized in unexpected ways. Share your dashed dreams with your kids. Discuss how God repurposed those dreams to fit His purpose for your life, just like He did with Joseph in Genesis 37–50. Joseph's dreams were not wrong, they just were not fulfilled until he experienced the pit, the prison, and the palace. The situation, the timing, and the necessary character growth had to line up for his dreams to come to fruition.

My daughter Samantha and her husband Alex applied flexible thinking to their living situation when their plans to move to New York were indefinitely suspended due to the coronavirus. They planned to relocate from San Francisco to New York. Both Samantha and Alex were ready for a new adventure. Samantha quit her job in preparation for the move. Then came Covid-19. New York locked down. Alex's company delayed their plans to open an office in the Big Apple. It looked as if this relocation may not occur for another year. New York was on hold, Samantha was out of work, and Alex was working remotely.

They stepped back for a minute and examined their living situation from a different perspective.

1. If Alex is working remotely, couldn't he work from anywhere?
2. If Samantha is out of a job, isn't she free to job hunt elsewhere?
3. If the long-term plan was to move to San Diego, why not now?

This set of circumstances became an opportunity. The couple regrouped. They packed up their belongings and put them in storage. Samantha secured a new job where she works remotely. And they moved into an apartment in Pacific Beach.

Flexible thinking allowed them to see the unrealized New York plan made space for a new and improved dream. Here are a few biblical stories that depict an out-of-the-box solution. In these stories the people problem-solved and trusted God in their circumstances. These are great stories to share and discuss with our kids.

1. While trusting God, Baby Moses' mom placed him in the river to keep him safe (Exodus 2).
2. Against all odds, Joshua and Caleb trusted God with the timing of entering the Promised Land (Numbers 14).
3. Young David slays Goliath, the over nine-foot-tall Philistine (1 Samuel 17).

Problems like the ones Moses' mom, Joshua, Caleb, and David encountered were impossible to solve without God. Practice flexible thinking with your kids. Do a puzzle or present a problem to be solved. Play games that encourage creative thinking.

God is teaching me that hard choices are places where hope can be discovered and creative thinking practiced. Bad choices and their consequences are opportunities for hope to shine. Times that include waiting are moments when God's glory is most evident.

Hope Busters
Impulsivity.
Impatience.
Inflexibility.

Hope Builders
Train your kids in delayed gratification to reduce impulsive acts.
Share your dashed dreams with your kids and how God redeemed those times.

Provide experience in flexible thinking and problem solving.

Hopeful Truths
Hope has an opportunity to shine in the hard choices.
God's timing is perfect.
God's ways are not my ways.

Prayer

Father, You are in, through, and above time. With You, a day is like a thousand years and a thousand years is like a day. Give my children and me the ability to persevere, think creatively, trust You, and in the process have hope in the distractions, dashed dreams, disappointments, delays, and dead ends. Show me Your way and help me to hold my plans loosely. Your way is the best eternal path. Amen.

> For no matter how many promises God has made, they are "Yes" in Christ. And so through him the "Amen" is spoken by us to the glory of God.
> —2 Corinthians 1:20

Chapter 2

SUFFERING STINKS

Brothers and sisters, we do not want you to be uninformed about those who sleep in death, so that you do not grieve like the rest of mankind, who have no hope.

—1 Thessalonians 4:13

As a newly married couple, Tom and I lived the happy predictable life. We graduated from college. Check. He got a job as an accountant. I got a job as a teacher. Check, check. We got married. Check. We planned well. We did it right. Heck, unlike many of our contemporaries, we even went to church.

We decided to broaden our spiritual horizons and join a three-year Bible study. The study took the participants through the entire Bible. We were the youngest members of the class. Most of the class members were the age we are now. Many were parents of young adult children. Some were even grandparents. Our one-year anniversary had just been celebrated. At the time, becoming a parent was just a dream.

Stories of broken relationships, health concerns, and financial struggles were shared by most. Tom and I listened in discomfort and disbelief at the heartache and hardship many had endured. We determined the messy journey in which our fellow Bible students had found themselves would not be our path. After all, we were good people. We did things right. We thoughtfully planned. Check, check, check.

"What did they do wrong?" I silently mused.

I don't recall much of what I learned from the study of Scripture and theology during those three years. I can tell you the lesson the Lord had begun to press upon my heart, soul, and mind. Hope, true hope, born from trust and faith was what the Lord was teaching me. Not *the pull yourself up by your bootstraps* type of hope. Not good thoughts type of hope. Real hope found in Him.

My classmates' lives instructed me. Soon experience would be my teacher too. I began to understand, hope is not whimsical. The culture's hope which consists of good vibes, good thoughts, and a good attitude has zero power. True hope is bold power and strength.

Only a few months after joining the study Tom and I experienced the unexpected sudden death of his dad, followed by years of infertility. Hope grew in our innocent suffering.

As our life goes on, we realize it will continue to be untidy. Like our former fellow Bible students, it has been filled with David and Goliath type of challenges related to family, finances, jobs, and health. Dreams may be pushed away but God draws us close.

Disaster

My friend Emily Scott and her family faced a giant-sized challenge too. Their Goliath came in the form of a fire.

Emily wrote these words in her blog, "Unfortunately, many children must face devastating events during their childhood. Thankfully, these events don't have to be as tragic and disheartening as they often seem. Our family experienced this firsthand when we lost our home in the 8th largest wildfire in California history. The Carr Fire destroyed almost 1100 homes in July 2018.

"Although this tragedy was a difficult thing to experience, we were fortunate to be able to walk with our children through the experience. We have been asked many times how we parented through such an event. We parented as consistently and as normally as the situation would allow, we parented with empathy, we allowed our children to be sad, and more than anything, we parented with hope and confidence that we could all form resilience from tragedy."[7]

Hope, when it is birthed from tragedy, often shows up in the form of security. Security for kids is defined by consistency and normalcy. Emily recommends, "Get back to normal as soon as you can. For us, after our home was destroyed, we had to live in a hotel for two weeks and then moved into a rental house. Our life was chaos for several months as we started rebuilding and trying to find our new normal. But whatever aspects of life we could get 'normal' we did. Our daughter still attended dance camp the following week. We still went swimming at the hotel pool and Grandpa's house. We parented as close to normal as the situation allowed."[8]

Chris and Emily Scott offered hope when they talked with their kids about the facts of the fire. They were open and available to their children. They were open to their questions and created opportunities to share feelings about the loss. The couple was keenly aware that the way they responded to this tragedy would make a lasting impression on their children. They kept the dialogue open, allowed the kids to grieve, remained calm, and let their children see them grieve, feel sad, and be frustrated. With their kids, they discussed plans for a new home. The children saw their parents ask for and accept help. Emily and Chris were sensitive to their children's developmental stage, knowing younger kids may cry or be irritable while teens might isolate. Uniqueness in personalities was also respected; some wanted to talk about the trauma and others wanted to shut the event out of their mind.

Healthy coping skills and a trust in God's goodness were modeled by this couple. Their children learned even in the hard times, there is still hope. It has been two years since the fire. The Scott's home is rebuilt and life is back to normal. In her blog Emily writes, "After loss or a tragic event, kids can feel powerless, afraid, sad, lonely, that life isn't fair, and many other emotions. All of these are valid and OK. How we [parents] respond to them is what's important."[9]

Devastating News

Unwelcome health issues like physical maladies or developmental issues can unexpectedly invade our lives. Instantly, they appear out of nowhere. My friend, Anne, has a young adult son who was in a snowboard accident. He is paralyzed and wheelchair bound.

Anne stated, "According to the doctors, my son has beaten the odds."

Trent has miraculously regained some movement. Anne attributes his progress to a strong will, prayer, a supportive and encouraging wife and family, plus a determined physical therapist. He can stand and use his arms. He is an amazing young man with a strong spirit. He embodies a hope-filled outlook and a hopeful life.

Trent has participated in his progress, just as the blind man in John 9:6–7 needed to be actively involved in his healing. Jesus "spit on the ground, made some mud with the saliva, and put it on the man's eyes. 'Go,' he told him, 'wash in the Pool of Siloam' (this word means 'Sent'). So the man went and washed, and came home seeing."

Hope is not a passive quality. Often the Lord invites or directs us to actively partner with Him.

Disillusionment

There are times the path a person is on will bring them to a destination that other family members may not want to travel. This is the case for my friend Diane and her children.

Against her adult children's wishes, Diane filed for divorce after over thirty years of marriage. This decision did not come easily nor quickly. Many conversations, counseling, and prayer occurred.

Twice over the thirty years, the couple separated. "I chose to separate for the children's protection and safety. There was one night where my husband was so angry, I thought he might kill me."

They would reconcile but the cycle of addiction continued to mar and mark their married life. There was no financial or sexual trust. No social or recreational unity.

"There was nothing to hang my hat on. It took a lot for me to realize, I had to jump off this cliff. This was the place where I needed ultimate trust in God."

She went on to say, "I counted the cost of the loss of family time, the loss of a future sharing grandkids. This was agonizing, I did not want to make a mistake. I moved methodically and slowly with each decision. I was open to where God wanted me. The loss of the dream of what the relationship could be was the final nail in the coffin. I realized I was pursuing a dream and not living in reality.

"I asked myself, 'Do I want to go through these decade-long cycles in my sixties, seventies, and eighties just because my adult children wanted us to stay married?' I needed to make my own decision, with the realization divorce would blow up the family system."

Diane did divorce the father of her children. In hindsight she wishes she had spoken these words to her kids, "This is the hardest thing we will go through as a family. I still believe God is good. He will create a new family constellation and we will find a new way to communicate and relate."

Diane is now hopeful regarding her own future. The hope she offers her adult children is one of commitment to her relationship with them and a willingness to talk and resolve conflict as it occurs. Two of her young adults have stepped forward in this new family system with her. The third struggles with the divorce, yet is as committed to staying connected to her mom as her mom is to her.

Even when family life no longer looks like what it used to, hope says, "When the family shifts, we can find a new way to be a family. All is not lost; we can find a new way together."

Diane says, "I believe in marriage and place a high value on it. Maybe that is why it was so hard to come to this decision. I don't regret divorcing my husband."

Diane knows why God hates divorce; it is a painful experience for all involved. She also sees why God allows it in the case of addiction, abuse, affair, or abandonment. In her case, hope is found in the healing.

The Way Prepared

Hope can be found in emotional healing. What happens to hope when physical healing does not occur?

Death is normal, natural, and inevitable. It has no boundaries and lays claim to all living creatures. Our kids, ready or not, will be affected by it. We can help them by wrapping the hope we have in Jesus and the eternal life He guarantees.

Understanding death is a critical component of our children's emotional development. Childhood is the time to equip them with the tools needed to deal with loss.

Tragic death entered my ninth-grade son's world when Eric, one of Jake's best buddies, was killed in a car accident freshman year. In middle school, Kendra experienced the death of a friend, too. As did Courtney, her freshman year. Three of my four teenage kids lost a friend in a car accident. All three needed hope, the hope eternal life offers.

I knew hope was the thing my kids needed. I was unsure how to offer it. I was at a loss. "Lord, what is the best way to help my kids?" I prayed.

Listening and offering hugs seemed to be what the girls needed. My son needed reassurance.

"Mom, we never talked about faith."

"Jake, I could see Eric had faith. I could tell by the light in his eyes."

"You don't know that, Mom." I did have that confidence. My son thought I was trying to make him feel better.

I prayed a wimpy prayer, "Lord, *just* give Jake peace in this situation, Amen."

I got a call from Eric's mom, Mette, a few weeks after Eric's death.

"An assistant principal just delivered a packet of papers from Eric's classes. An assignment from his English class was in the envelope. Eric told me about this. He said he had written something about himself. He was excited about it. I just read it. I feel like I am meant to share this with Jake. I know Jake is a spiritual person and I think he would find comfort in this. I want Jake to know, Eric is OK."

Jake and I zipped over to Mette's home. Jake needed to see Eric's words for himself. The assignment was titled, "I wonder." In Eric's handwriting were the words, "I wonder when I will die and see the light of Christ." Eric penned that a couple of days before the accident.

The God of the Universe beckoned a grieving mom to Himself and gave comfort to a fourteen-year-old boy all at once. Eric, in his own words, written in his own hand, reassured Jake. As Mette says, "This was a spiritual thing." God can speak through impossible circumstances.

I was uncomfortable with my kids experiencing such deep grief. Those deaths shook my world and broke my mom-heart too. They were a stark reminder our life can change in an instant and that earth is not our home.

The Talk

In our 21st century western culture, death is more removed. It most often occurs in hospitals and nursing homes. Long ago people died at home surrounded by loved ones.

Today, death seems more mysterious and younger kids are curious. At my grandmother's funeral my younger cousin declared, "She blinked!" when peering into the open casket. It takes time for children to grasp the idea that physical death is a permanent state of being.

When you talk with your young child about death be:

1. Specific
2. Clear
3. Concise
4. Honest
5. Empathic
6. Available
7. Approachable

8. Normal
9. Aware
10. Sensitive

Specific. Use the "D" words. Death, Died, Dying, Dead. If the child is attending a funeral service, tell him how the event will unfold. Describe what he will see and hear using a timeline as your guide. "When we get to the funeral home you could hear some people crying. They are sad. You will see____ in a coffin. Then we will listen to the pastor and sing some songs. After that . . ."

Clear. Avoid the use of euphemisms like passed on, lost, transitioned, gone home, and eternal slumber. State it simply, "She died."

Concise. Don't say she died because she was sick. If the person was sick say, "She was really *big* sick. Not regular sick (sore throat, flu, cold)." If the death was due to a disease, name it. "She had a disease called cancer. The cancer made her body *big* sick, not regular sick."

Honest. Do say, "I feel sad. I will miss Grandpa." This gives your child permission to grieve. Bring Jesus into the conversation. Discuss how He felt sad when His friend Lazarus died ("Jesus wept," John 11:1–37).

Empathic. Normalize your child's feelings by sharing memories of your feelings when you were your child's age and you experienced a loss. "I remember when I was seven years old and my dog died. I was sad, just like you are sad about our dog." Let the child know it is OK to have happy moments during sad times. Laughter and fun are not a betrayal. Having joyful times reminiscing about the deceased is one way to honor their life and legacy.

Available. Little ones need to feel secure, comforted, and reassured. It is critical for kids to know their parents love them, are there for them, and are willing to help them get through the hard times. "We will help each other. Things will get better."

Approachable. The topic of death is almost taboo. Your child needs to know it is good to talk and to ask questions about death. Answer with honesty and simplicity. "How will Grandpa eat (go to the bathroom, wake up, move, breathe, talk, feel) when he's dead?" "He won't eat (go to the bathroom, wake up, move, breathe, talk, feel) when he's dead because his body doesn't work anymore." Follow up with, "God gives us a new body in Heaven." If a child asks a question a parent does not have the answer to, admit it. "I don't know the answer to your question. I have wondered the same thing."

Normal. Maintain your routine as much as possible while being sensitive to your child's needs. You may need to make some temporary adjustments to your child's schedule. Extra down time, snuggle time, or quality time with mom or dad may be necessary.

Aware. Understand your child's developmental stage. Preschoolers are in the magical thinking stage. They believe wishes make things happen. Kids at this age may be especially fearful. Death is viewed as reversible and temporary. Children ages five to nine realize death is final but not personal. They think conceptually and recognize others' emotions. To comprehend hard information, kids at this age need it repeated frequently. In the tween and teen years, kids fully understand death is irreversible and know they will die someday.

Sensitive. Kids react differently and find comfort in different things. Some cry, others become angry, some clingy, others whiney. Some may act as if nothing has happened while others find solace in reading, drawing, writing, listening to music, or playing. No matter how your child copes with death or expresses his feelings, he needs sympathetic and nonjudgmental responses from his parents. Study your child so you can respond accordingly. If you see signs of intense fear, the inability to sleep or eat, or if the child appears to carry the weight of the world on his shoulders, you may want to seek professional help.

Possible actions parents can take to celebrate a deceased loved one's life are:

1. Create a book of memories to help keep the deceased person or pet alive in our kid's mind. The goal is to

accept the death bit by bit and recall the importance of the relationship and person (or animal).

2. Light a candle in memory of your loved one. Talk about how Jesus lights the way for us.

3. Attend the funeral —if you feel your child is ready and he wants to attend.

4. Hold a funeral. If a pet has died, have a family memorial service.

5. Help or serve others. Give your child a job so he can see what comforting another person looks like.

6. With your tweens and young adults, be available to sit with them in the pain. Listen. Avoid saying, "I know how you feel." Just be there.

7. If your kids are receptive, here are some verses to read that may bring comfort. Emphasize those who know Christ will be with Him rather than those who do not know Christ will perish: John 11:25–26; 14:1-3; Romans 8:38; Philippians 1:21; 1 Thessalonians 4:13–18; Revelation 21:4.

No matter the child's age, spend time together. They need reassurance that they are safe and loved. Be available for them to ask questions and discuss feelings about death. Be clear and concise when talking about death. Model how to put emotions into words. Describe what to expect. Respond to your child's emotions, comfort him yet do not stay stuck on the sad feelings. A distraction or change of venue may be called for. The grieving process is a little different for everyone. Grieving takes time.

Grief Places

Our kiddos need to explore their feelings so they can understand what their emotions teach them about themselves and what they value. Connection plus time for emotional healing helps our kids move to problem-solving mode and develop emotional coping mechanisms.

Connection is the first response to your child's grief. In my book, *The Messy Life of Parenting*, empathy versus sympathy is discussed and defined, "Empathy says, 'I'm here with you in this hard place.' Sympathy speaks, 'I'm sorry you are in that hard place.'"[10] Sympathy disconnects while empathy connects.

The Messy Life of Parenting goes on to list six progressive stages of response to help the child navigate and cope with difficult moments: Experience it, express it, define it, deal with it, learn from it, and use it.[11]

Before we can get to the place where God can use our pain to help another, we find ourselves in some hard places. I believe the stages of grief are really more like places of grief. Places where we sit for a period of time. These spots may be revisited. My experience tells me grief does not move through consecutive stages. Instead it camps at various locations like denial, anger, depression, bargaining, and acceptance.[12] Some spots may house one longer than others.

Even though it is painful to watch our kids grieve, don't fear the sadness. In my book, *Messy Journey: How Grace Offers the Prodigal a Way Home*, grief is characterized as an expression of love. "Grieving is good. It is the beginning of healing and moving forward."[13]

Grieve Well

We can do things that acknowledge the grief while celebrating a life when a loved one has passed. My Uncle Don, my mom's brother, died from a heart attack at the young age of fifty-three in 1989.

My mom, Pat (or Trish as her brother would call her), and I traveled to Bonita Springs, Florida to visit Auntie Carol, my mom's sister-in-law, in March, just prior to the country shutting down for the coronavirus. My aunt's fourth-floor condo at the Ambassador has a bird's-eye view of the gulf. When you look out her family room window or walk the beach you see a variety of birds: egrets, herons, spoonbills, and pelicans, to name a few. Dolphin sightings are common. Each night brings a spectacular and unique sunset.

Most folks will miss one of the sights that is most precious to my aunt and our family. It's a tall, thirty-year-old palm tree. It is planted right next to the condominium's wooden walkway to the beach. It provides much needed shade from the hot Florida sun. This tree has survived a number of hurricanes. It stands strong yet moves with the wind.

This palm tree was planted to commemorate the life of my uncle, my mom's brother, my aunt's husband. Every day my aunt views this special tree from her bay window. Seeing it provides her and those who loved my uncle with a sense of joy, comfort, and hope. It reminds us of his life, his contagious laugh, the twinkle in his eye, and his quick wit. We recall how he made each of us feel special when we were in his presence.

Physical items are tangible things that give a sense of comfort and hope. Tom's dad died just prior to Uncle Don's passing. He had a massive and fatal heart attack. It was devastating and completely unexpected. His death left a big hole in the family. Following his November heart attack, Tom wore his dad's trench coat or leather bomber jacket almost daily. They brought my husband comfort in the loss.

I get it. I have one of my dad's Up North Sweatshirts. My dad's favorite place was the cabin, up north (as Minnesotans would say) at Rabbit Lake. Wearing that blue, scoop neck, cozy sweatshirt feels like a hug.

To help your child in the grieving process, find some sort of tangible thing to wear, see, or even smell to bring comfort to a hurting soul. Avoid rushing grief. Rather than dismiss feelings, embrace them, and celebrate the life of the loved one. Remembrance brings hope. "I thank my God every time I remember you" (Philippians 1:3).

"I was married to Marty for forty-one years. His death was a shock. He had not been sick; he was in great shape. Even the paramedics said he was in excellent shape. A brain aneurysm caused his heart to stop. I praise God in this storm. I praise Him that I was married to a really good man for forty-one years. I thank the Lord for that time. I want to keep my focus on the Lord and have an attitude of thanks and praise."[14] —Sandy

Not everyone can handle the loss of a loved one with the same attitude of gratefulness. Death can be the open door to a faith-based conversation. Pray for God's words and wisdom before approaching your child. Ask God if this is the time to retell the Easter story.

"My brother was homeless, he struggled with addiction, and died from diabetes. But God was evident in my brother's last days. In one of his final conversations with loved ones he said, 'I'm working on getting permanent housing.'" His sister, Jill, finds comfort in his words. Her homeless brother is in his permanent eternal home. Death is not the end but a new beginning.

> We are confident, I say, and would prefer to be away from the body and at home with the Lord.
> —2 Corinthians 5:8

Hope Busters
Passivity.
Protection from pain.
Pushing past grief.

Hope Builders
Maintain as much consistency and normalcy in times of tragedy or loss.
Be available to listen to your children share their hearts amid suffering.
Be honest and share your sadness with your children.

Hopeful Truths
Sadness is a part of life and it is temporary.
We have eternal life in Christ.
Grief is an expression of love, not to be hidden or feared.

Prayer

Lord God, everyone will have times of suffering in their lives. My children are not immune from hardship or heartache. Help me to show them how to walk through troubled times with hope. Let them see I have my eyes fixed on You. Amen.

> After his suffering, he presented himself to them and gave many convincing proofs that he was alive. He appeared to them over a period of forty days and spoke about the kingdom of God.
> —Acts 1:3

Chapter 3

HARD WORLD

But those who suffer he delivers in their suffering;
he speaks to them in their affliction.

—Job 36:15

Horrified, I sat on my couch watching the news as the video streamed high school kids dropping out of second story windows to escape the killing spree going on inside Columbine High School. My stomach tightened when I realized the location of the school was Littleton, Colorado.

Littleton was the town where my husband's apartment resided. In January of 1999 Tom secured a job with Sports Authority at their headquarters in Englewood. We had plans to move the family from Minnesota to Colorado at the end of July.

We moved to Colorado after Columbine. There was no "before Columbine" in our children's Colorado experience. School, church, and movie theater shootings are realities they grew up with. Praise God they never personally experienced any of this violence. They have been reminded of the violence due to school lockdown drills.

Clement Park Lake Trail is a 1.7-mile loop that circles Johnson Reservoir. On the east side of the reservoir is a hill where the Columbine Memorial is located, several hundred yards west of the school. Clement Park is a place frequented by many who live in Southwest Denver.

My friend Darcy and I often walk that trail. My son attended and graduated from Columbine High School. The memory and impact of April 20, 1999 is still felt in the community. The tragedy was over twenty years ago.

In the film, *We are Columbine*, students and educators were interviewed. The question was asked, "When did school get back to normal?"

Frank DeAngelis, Columbine Principal, said, "It never did. We had to redefine what normal is." A former Columbine student—wiping tears from her eyes as her voice shook—said, "Feeling safe—I think it had a new definition after the shooting. Just kinda doing the best you can every day."[15] Columbine survivors had to redefine what normal and safety looked like.

Our kids are growing up in a hard world. Yet, it does not have to be a hopeless one. We can arm them with hope for their future.

Racial Healing in a Hard World

Most people were shocked and deeply disturbed by the video depicting George Floyd's knee to the neck death in Minneapolis on May 25, 2020. People of all colors felt concern over this. Most folks hope to bridge the racial divide and desire healing. Hope can be found in the hard and horrible when we seek to understand each other. Maybe in these terrible moments we can see opportunities for healing and change.

Only within the last six years or so have I realized mothers and fathers coach their black sons on society's unwritten rules for black men. Author and speaker Sheila Qualls offers her perspective in her blog titled, "A New View on Race from a Mother's Heart" on normalcy, safety, race, and her family's experience.

> The tragic death of George Floyd cut me deep. As I watched Floyd cry out for help and struggle to breathe, I couldn't help but think . . . that could've been one of my sons.
>
> It doesn't matter that they're from a middle-class, two-parent home. It doesn't matter that they're educated and articulate.
>
> People see their black skin first.

Racism is real. I've felt its sting. I've been trailed through stores. Shop owners have asked to search my purse. Tellers have eyed me with suspicion when I've withdrawn my own money from the bank.

I know humiliation, but I also know truth. I refuse to let the actions of a few taint my view of the world. George Floyd's death was unjust, tragic and unnecessary. Still, I don't believe most white people are racist.

As the mother of black sons, I had to coach my boys on society's unwritten rules for Black men. What they should and shouldn't wear, how to treat others, how to act with dignity, and how to speak confidently. I also taught them they're not victims, and a victim mentality will limit them economically and emotionally.

I can't tell them race doesn't matter after the death of George Floyd. I can't tell them race doesn't matter when they've been repeatedly pulled over by police who are 'randomly' checking vehicles in the predominantly white areas we've lived in.

I can tell them where I stand. First, they're responsible for themselves, their families, and their communities. Second, they're bound by the rules of society and the law, which I know they'll respect. I've raised them to be men of character and integrity.

I can tell them their father and I believe America is the best place in the world. Is it perfect? No. Even so, they have an opportunity to be beacons of hope and examples of what is best about this country.[16]

Many want to stand up to racism and are unsure how. Sheila offers nine ways to combat racism and move toward healing.

1. Instead of trying to be politically correct, focus on being biblically correct.
2. Know history, but don't be manipulated by it.
3. Identify a safe person and ask questions to open dialog.

4. Talk to your children and shape their perspective.
5. Listen without taking offense.
6. Challenge your paradigm and help someone challenge theirs by getting outside your comfort zone.
7. Examine your thoughts and attitudes in relation to God's word.
8. Support programs and organizations that are rooted in biblical principles and uphold American values.
9. Encourage personal responsibility, regardless of color.[17]

"We don't have to find new solutions for racism. Jesus has already given us timeless ones. Judge others by their character not their color. Treat everyone—regardless of race, social stature, or religious affiliation—with respect, compassion, and dignity. Allow others to see the fullness of Christ by being the best you can be."[18]

Hope for Healing

Nina is one of my most trusted and loyal friends. We talk about deep things, hard things. She's black. I'm white. We are able to listen, consider, and pray together.

"Are you feeling without hope during these times?" I was concerned about my friend.

"No, I feel like this time is an eye-opening moment. I don't feel hopeless, instead it's a window of opportunity."

"How has God moved you to respond?"

"I am connecting with all the young black and brown men in my life. The Lord reminded me of Isaiah 50:4, a verse that has been my life mission. These words reverberated in my mind— *He has given me an instructed tongue to know the word that sustains the weary.* I am encouraging these men to gather and share their feelings and stories. I'm asking them, 'Why were you born during this time? What is your purpose?' We are collectively in mourning. When a killing of a black or brown man occurs, we feel like it has happened to a close friend. We personalize it, 'That could be my brother, my nephew, my son.' We see ourselves as if that could be one of us."

Nina has tenderly shown me an additional perspective. I understand a little more why each tragedy impacts the black and brown community so personally, so strongly. The feeling of family and connection to those of the same color is a strong bond. As Nina says, hard things can open up opportunities for better things.

Opportunity

Hard things can create opportunities for growth and increase resiliency. The pandemic has been one of those hard things that has the potential to be an opportunity for growth. This generation of kids, elementary through college-aged students have been forced to be flexible. They are learning to creatively manage their lives. These kids hold onto hope in a whole new way. That doesn't mean that frustration, anger, or irritation won't occur. In fact, it will. As our kids (and we) stretch, resistance is typically the first emotion felt and expressed.

Hope does not extinguish emotional expression. This is a truth worth remembering. Our kids can have hope and still experience struggles. Following an emotional meltdown, when our kids are ready to receive it, we can encourage them to problem solve by asking, "What action can you take to improve your situation and lessen your frustration?" Allowing our kids to move from frustration to problem solving is an empowering act.

The Line

There are those times we have no clue how we can make life better. When the world feels harsh, sometimes we just let it go or we cross the line and become an active participant. Are we numb to disrespect and unkindness?

In a hard world, people are selfish and want their way. They may go to extreme measures to get it, like terrorism, rioting, or bullying. Or they may choose more subtle measures like punishment or manipulation to achieve their goal.

Social media tends to be a place that is open to people punishing or ridiculing others for not thinking the way they think. Arguing, attacking, mocking, and calling names fill the posts and comments. Our kids watch the social discord, observing how we respond to differing points of view. I have witnessed believers and nonbelievers on both sides, behave unkindly. God's heart must break.

Have we lost the ability to tolerate a variety of points of view and beliefs? Several families I work with have young adults who threaten to cut off relationship due to differing politics.

I have had a similar experience. A woman I have known since she was twelve (she is now approaching forty), has been special to me and to our family. On social media she appears angry all the time. She trolls those she perceives to disagree with her on political issues and then puts on her boxing gloves and grabs her megaphone.

She used to be fun-loving and joyful. Her smile was big and bright. What happened? Over the last few years, her causes have become her idol.

She is not alone in this behavior. Whatever occupies our thoughts and time is an idol. That idol can get in the way of our relationships if we let it. We can treat others the way we want to be treated, no matter their race, religion, or political view. We just need to do it.

Our kids see the riots and the rage. What they are not witnessing is the way to effectively address hard things. The public discord has a dark cloud of hopelessness hovering over it.

We can do better, even in a world that feels as if it has spun out of control. In a hard world, our kids need to understand how to put appropriate boundaries in place and build a relationship bridge. In disagreement we can be respectful and seek understanding. It is OK if we do not agree. It is not OK if we cannot be respectful.

I have had to stop social media participants who want to use my personal feed and platform for their message and agenda. The younger woman I referred to earlier was not able to respect my boundaries. She cut ties with me because I removed her inflammatory comment.

On the bright side, setting social media expectations has worked well with my MOMS Together group. I put out a post stating, "At MOMS Together we focus on what draws us together (our mom role and love for our kids), we appreciate the diversity and differences in the way other moms' parent, we trust that each mom is who she needs to be for the children God has given her. If a mom wants to discuss politics, she can find that outlet on other social media platforms, MOMS Together is not one of them."

This idea can be transferred to the family. I recommend these guidelines to my parenting clients. Tweens to adults can learn to be respectful even in disagreement.

1. Expect respect. Table the discussion if needed until respect can be put into place.
2. Use I statements. I think, I believe, I feel.
3. Avoid name-calling.
4. State facts.
5. Avoid hyperbole, don't say: always, never.
6. Stay on topic (avoid tossing in that ol' kitchen sink).
7. Stay current (don't be a historian).
8. Discuss don't debate.
9. Listen rather than lecture.
10. Have a dialogue not a monologue.

If these boundaries are not abided by, the conversation needs to come to a halt. The manipulative or bullying tactics used by some are distracting at best and harmful at worst. They may sound like this: "You are overreacting." "You are so sensitive." "Settle down." "I was just kidding." "You are so difficult." "Come on, have a sense of humor." "Chill out."

These phrases are intended to throw you off the topic of concern and move you away from the boundaries you have put into place. Do not be distracted by them.

Guidelines are important, they support integrity. Boundaries are critical, they secure respect. Both guidelines and boundaries set the stage for hope in difficult relationships.

Invisible Boundaries

People pleasers are relationship seekers. They have difficulty setting boundaries. Many who suffer from anxiety tend to be people pleasers.

The hard world of the achievement culture adds to the need of pleasers to say yes to more responsibilities. Being overcommitted and overscheduled increases anxious thoughts, "I can't believe I agreed to this, I don't have time for this now."

Learn to say your best yes. This is challenging if you do not know your own needs. There are many good things, but not all good things are God's assignment for us.

Boundaries are for the boundary setter. They clearly express how one wants to be treated, they provide a structure for an individual to determine their needs, wants, and create a framework to live out faith and values. Those who do not respect boundaries are angered by those who have them and abide by them.

Boundary setting can be overdone. Unhealthy boundaries are inflexible and rigid. These boundaries are created from a selfish perspective, putting one person's needs above everyone else's. Unhealthy boundaries do not allow for grace, flexibility, or the human factor. They are solely focused on one individual's needs instead of considering the group at large. Some people wield boundaries like a weapon used to punish or shame another person.

When a person requests a favor and you have a catch in your spirit, it is OK to ponder and wait. If you are unsure say, "It sounds interesting, I need to give this some thought." Look at how practical it is to say yes and then decide. The extra time will give you a moment to consider this.

When I am asked to do a task regarding ministry, my heart is to say yes. This can be problematic; no boundary setting causes overcommitment. Wishy-washy and inconsistent boundaries inadvertently invite others to ignore them. Poor boundary setting looks like this:

1. Unable to say no because you do not want to disappoint someone.
2. You say yes when you really want to say no.
3. You pretend to agree even when you disagree.
4. You vacillate on making a choice or have trouble making a decision.
5. You are unable to speak up, even when your feelings have been hurt.
6. You feel as if you are being used or taken advantage of.
7. Believe everyone's happiness is your responsibility.
8. Give away too much of yourself, your time, your resources and feel frustrated with that.
9. Here's a secret I have discovered, I can say no and people will still like me. (Crazy huh?)

Saying no sounds like this: "Oh wow, that sounds really great but I'm not able to commit to that." "I'd like to say yes because I believe you have an important mission. The task isn't in my wheelhouse of strengths, so I need to say no." "I don't want to disappoint you but I'm unable to fit that into my schedule." "Thank you for asking but I have to say no. It won't work out for me."

People pleasers have trouble getting their own needs met and feel powerless and helpless. When they reach their breaking point, aggression, passive aggression, addiction, or avoidance may become their coping mechanism.

Setting and implementing boundaries is respectful resistance. The skill that helps achieve this is assertiveness, the ability to be one's own advocate.

The signs aggression rather than assertiveness is occurring sounds a lot like blame: "You made me do that." "It's all your fault." "You never do anything." "I hate you." "You always mess up."

Passive aggression is meanness cloaked in niceness. The anger that is felt comes out indirectly, "I'm not mad. I'm just used to this." "You sure seem to care about everyone else but me. But that's OK." "Fine. Do whatever you want." "You are so busy. I know you don't have time for me."

Often a passive-aggressive person includes other toxic communication patterns like an eye roll, sarcasm, guilt trip, or the silent treatment.

Frustration and anger, when dealt with in unhealthy ways, come out as passive-aggressive swings, aggressive blasts, or acting out.

"My eight-year-old son resorts to antagonizing his brothers, when he feels frustrated."—Janelle

Train your kids to express anger and their needs in a non-sinful way. It is possible to speak up and assert personal needs without being hurtful. Using one's voice to state a concern or need generates hope.

Assertiveness and self-advocacy sound like this: "I feel_____, when you _____." "I get you have a lot happening. Yet I feel unsupported." "What just occurred is not OK. Help me understand what is going on." "I'd love to get together. I value our time together." "I'm sad you can't attend but I understand."

Real World

The real world our kids live in includes violence. Sociocultural fear factors like terrorist attacks, racial tension, school shootings, lockdowns, gun violence, political discord, and high-profile suicides add to children's potential angst and hopelessness. Toss in the achievement culture, parental anxiety, social comparison, smartphone usage, social media, and Covid-19, and you can see how fear and anxiety enter our kids' brains and emotions.

Therapists Jason Daugherty and Kelly Martin say, "Real threats can lead to cognitive distortion and adolescents don't have enough life experience to know the difference between risk and inevitability."[19] A heightened sense of fear encourages exaggerated reactions. Negative and hopeless thoughts can be challenged. Reality and probability can quell some imagined fear.

Ask:

1. Am I totally certain of this? Thoughts and feelings are not facts.
2. Is there evidence against these negative thoughts? Look to see if the thoughts are real, imagined, or a pattern you may have.
3. Do others see it this way? Do a reality check and ask someone else their opinion or thoughts.
4. Are these thoughts worth expending all this energy? Negativity zaps energy. Positivity creates energy.
5. Do I want to change my negative perspective? We need to want to alter thought patterns to adjust a negative line of thinking to a positive one.

"I'm not naturally a super optimistic person. The waves of hard things kept coming: my husband had an affair, lost his job, I began drinking to cope which only made things worse. I could not even stand before another situation knocked me down. I wish I could say I go straight to hope or faith in times of crisis. I don't. What helps me is separating fact from feeling and the thought, 'I can get through this. I have a choice, to fight or not.'"[20] —Jodie

Soften the Hard World

Our kids have a lot to navigate as they make their way through this crazy, chaotic, and complicated world. Determining fact from feeling is more important than optimism. Fact: My husband lost his job. Feeling: I feel afraid because my husband lost his job. The facts define the problem to be solved.

Our homes can be a soft place to land. In *The Messy Life of Parenting*, the topic of being an emotionally safe home is discussed. Here are some self-examination questions for moms and dads to consider. (Keep in mind, we all struggle and fall short. Also remember we can all raise the emotionally safe bar.)

1. Am I trustworthy with confidential information?
2. Am I sensitive to personal struggles and hopes shared?
3. Do I refrain from using personal information as a weapon later?
4. Am I able to handle small irritations and inconveniences in life with calm and patience?
5. Do I remain calm when bad decisions are made or accidents occur?
6. Do I avoid comparing my child to his or her siblings or peers?
7. Am I able to deal directly with a problem rather than use a passive-aggressive approach?
8. Can I be kind even when I disagree?
9. Do I let my children express their opinions and thoughts even if they are different from mine?
10. Am I real with my kids? Do I let them know I experience struggles and make mistakes?
11. Are my expectations realistic or perfection-based?
12. Is my home a place where it is OK to be less than perfect and a little weird sometimes?[21]

"After some honest self-examination, make the necessary adjustments. We can all do better. When our homes are built on respect, empathy, understanding, loyalty, trust, humility, grace, and unconditional love, we create an atmosphere where our children will share their struggles both big and small. We can't make them tell us their problems. We can do something better. We can foster a relationship where they want to invite us into their lives, telling us about their struggles and successes."[22]

Resilience Strengtheners

Our kids will go through times of both struggles and success. Resiliency in the struggles takes blood, sweat, and tears. It is a quality that grows in the hard places. If you are like me, you prefer the path of least resistance.

To ready us, God allows challenges so we can face tougher times down the road. Our kids learn resilience when they experience failure, disappointment, loss, or heartache. Bravery occurs when they face fear. Compassion grows through suffering. Anger can encourage problem solving. Persistence occurs when striving to reach a goal.

It is natural to want to prevent and protect our kids from heartache and hardship. It may be better for them to walk through these things when we are beside them. If we continue to protect our kids, they will believe they cannot handle struggle. Or they may even think they are entitled to a struggle-free life.

Emily Scott says this about letting our kids face challenges, "Helping our kids deal with the stress of life and the hardships of growing up is an important responsibility we have. When our children have practice managing stress and have a strong sense of resilience, they are better equipped to handle the difficulties life will throw at them as adults. Building resilience in them does not mean trying to toughen them up. It means working with them through struggles and being a source of loving, unconditional support."[23]

For your kiddos' sake, let them learn how strong they can be during tough times. Those moments are the best learning experiences. These are the times they can embrace hope by living in the *even if*, "*Even if* I don't_____ (make the team), I can still _____." *Even if* is faith-based thinking while *What if* is fear-based emotion.

Resilience allows us to bounce back from hard things that happen in a hard world. Here are some ways this character trait can be exercised:

1. Keep short accounts. Do not hold a grudge. Forgive. Try not to take things personally. Otherwise, you remain in victim mode, still thinking about the last offense while the other person has moved on. Many slights are unintentional, not meant to be a personal

attack. Most people usually think only of themselves and do not even consider you when making a decision. The action may never have been intended to be a personal attack or insult.

2. Hope for the best, be ready for the worst. Not in the sense of a fearful, "When will the next shoe drop?" but more along the lines of smart preparation in case things go sideways. Have a plan B.

3. Engage in an activity that you are not gifted at. You will need to step out of your comfort zone and persevere. This can build resiliency.

4. Learn from your failures and celebrate your successes.

Hope Busters
Selfishness.
Social media arguments.
Shutting down feelings.

Hope Builders
Encourage personal responsibility.
Connect with, listen, and dialogue with folks different from you (race, religion, politics).
Set boundaries and guidelines for social media and interpersonal interaction.

Hopeful Truths
We can disagree and still be respectful.
There are lots of good things but not all good things are God's assignments for us.
Boundaries are for the boundary setter.

Prayer

Father, You are a God of order, not of chaos. You are a God who is diverse within the Trinity. You sing over and delight in Your creation. Move us to cherish each other and this beautiful world You have created for us and given to us. Break our hearts for the things that break Yours. Amen.

> Not only so, but we also glory in our sufferings, because we know that suffering produces perseverance; perseverance, character; and character, hope. And hope does not put us to shame, because God's love has been poured out into our hearts through the Holy Spirit, who has been given to us.
>
> —Romans 5:3–5

Chapter 4

HOPE KILLERS

Sustain me, my God, according to your promise,
and I will live; do not let my hopes be dashed.
                                        —Psalm 119:116

"Things don't always turn out the way we want them to."
A nurse spoke these hope-killing words to me as my
unconscious, internally bleeding daughter was swept away on
a sheet-covered gurney to the operating room at St. Anthony
Hospital.

The hospital staff had begun to prep her for surgery, even
while she was being lifted out of the ambulance. Time was of
the essence.

Apparently, one of the nurses thought I did not understand
the gravity of the situation. To be sure I did she tossed some
insensitive reality my way. Thankfully, her comment, albeit
memorable, did not grab my heart. God was with me and I
knew He was with Kendra.

The nurse's words were intentional. Her message was
not prophetic. Things turned out just as I had hoped. Kendra
survived her snowboard accident.

I cannot speak to the nurse's intentions other than to wonder,
"Did she think she was helping me prepare for the worst?" Even
if that was her motivation, why say that? Dream-wrecker words
pop the hope bubble.

Our words can speak hope and victory or hopelessness
and defeat. That nasty nurse was a killer, a hope-killer.

Contrast and Compare

I have been a hope-killer. The times I compared my kiddo's strength or weakness to others, attempting to challenge and encourage them. That approach, it does not work. Just saying.

Hope-killers statements sound like this:

"Your brother spends more time studying. If you did that too your grades could be as good as his."

"Have you seen the way Braxton is so polite and helpful to his mom? I wish you would be like that."

"Don't worry about this so much. Just eat healthy and exercise, like your sister does."

The third comment was one I made to Kendra when she was in middle school and she was concerned about her weight. (For the record she was thin.)

My intention was to encourage and provide perspective. Instead, I stirred competition and contributed to Kendra's anxiety about food. She ended up with an eating disorder, which lasted a couple years. I added to the problem by discounting her worry and using her sister as an example. Comparison backfires.

Here is the comparison trajectory: Self-worth diminishes, jealousy is stirred, envy rises, resentment grows, bitterness takes over, discontent moves in, frustration with life fills the mind, anger at others and with God occurs. Comparison is relationship poison.

Most of us hope our kids will not just be siblings but also be good friends. We desire relationship over rivalry. We want our kids to grow to be the person God created them to be, not the clone of someone else. Comparison is a catalyst for hopelessness and a killer of relationships.

Comparison results in:

Giving up: "I could never be that good. I'm not even going to try."

Workaholism: "I'm going to strive harder than the other guy. I'm going to add more no matter the cost."

It sounds like:

"You love _____ more than me."

"He is your favorite."

"You spend more time with _____."

Relationships are all unique. People connect on different levels due to common interests and personalities. But love--love multiplies, it never divides.

Tom and I do our best to be there for each one of our kids and their spouses. There are seasons one may need more than another. It can be hard to balance when some live just minutes away and others across the country.

Comparison delivers the message of conditional love and adds to the current cultural thought of "you are not enough." Someone will always be better, smarter, stronger, or prettier. Someone will always have it easier or be healthier.

We can get stuck on that hamster wheel of self-improvement. There is nothing wrong with self-improvement if it does not become an idol. The caution is self-improvement can create feelings of either inadequacy or puffed-up pride.

God is always refining us. If our measuring stick is someone else's accomplishments or relationships, that is when it becomes problematic.

Comparison often produces insecurity which leads to self-pity, a woe-is-me attitude. The all-about-me mentality is entitled selfishness. Be aware when this type of thinking shows up in yourself or your kids. Perspective is needed.

We will never find complete satisfaction in our accomplishments, appearance, athleticism, academics, or abilities because the truth is we are human, imperfect beings, who have shortfalls, weaknesses, and inadequacies. We also have been gifted by God with skills and qualities that can reflect His glory.

Thankfulness and gratefulness change the comparison mindset. Self-pity and puffy pride disappear when an appreciative and content heart is magnified. Contentment and joy, for who God created us to be, fosters hope.

Confidence and Comparison

We compare when we lack confidence. We size things up and prove to ourselves we really are lacking. The positive side of comparison keeps us ready and willing to learn.

We get into trouble when we consistently compare ourselves to others who are more gifted or further along in the journey. Then the result is dissatisfaction, unworthiness, or even worthlessness.

Perhaps the comparison, competition, and confidence or lack thereof, is driven from a place of pride. Pride generated from an insecure need to prove to oneself and to others our station in life.

The antidote to lack of confidence may be humility. Humility is not low self-esteem, that is tied to pride, rather it is an honest assessment of one's strengths and weaknesses. It is the knowledge of who we are in comparison to God, not to others.

The closer I am to the Lord, the more I feel comfortable with His guidance and how He has gifted me and is growing me. Contentment comes to fruition when I participate in His will, with the talents and abilities He has given me.

Thanking God for the unique qualities, calling, and gifting He has chosen for each of us is not prideful; it is an honest assessment of who we are and how we have been created to glorify God. This is not pride, it is God-confidence.

When the comparison struggle emerges, ask, "Lord, show me how You have gifted me for such a time as this."

Stories of comparison are recorded in scripture: Cain and Abel (Genesis 4:1–16), Jacob and Esau (Genesis 25:19–34; 27:1–45), Leah and Rachel (Genesis 29:15–30:24), Saul and David (1 Samuel 13–15), the older brother and the prodigal son (Luke 15:11–32), and Peter and John (John 21:18–23).

To help combat jealousy our eyes need to be fixed on God, not ourselves or others. In the parable of the workers in Matthew 20:1–16, God reminds us of His grace and generosity. He chooses how to reward the workers, whether they worked a full day or just an hour. This can be looked at as either unfairness or more accurately as God's great grace and generosity.

Celebrating another's win fights against hope-killing envy. Happiness for others moves us out of that place of comparison.

If we can encourage and support others, we are more prepared to follow the unique plan God has for us.

Get Smart

We have a choice: doom and gloom or hope and opportunity. Realism and positivity can occur in tandem. Children who receive affirming, life-giving messages are more likely to confidently pursue God's purpose for their life.

There are many kids today who will not try something new because they fear failure or believe they are dumb. When we describe our kids' talents using the term "smarts," confidence grows.

Author Dr. Kathy Koch discusses eight unique smarts in her book, *8 Great Smarts*. She guides parents to see the quality of smart in a different light. She shows how some smarts naturally and quickly emerge while others need to be awakened. She believes all people have all eight smarts. She encourages parents not to classify their child as smart or not smart.

Dr. Kathy unpacks Dr. Howard Gardner's theory of multiple intelligences. This theory allows moms and dads to look beyond old proofs of grades and degrees to see evidence of smarts in their child's life.[24]

"When 'sitting at the potter's wheel' (Isaiah 64:8) and 'knitting us together in our mother's womb' (Psalm 139:13–14), God chose our unique combination of genes to develop His gift of multiple intelligences. He did this for you and each of your children. He chose which smarts would be strengths. He chose you as the parent. The nurture you provide matters."[25]

Here is a summarized definition of the eight smarts: Body smart: think and learn through movement and touch. Nature smart: think and learn with patterns. People smart: think and learn with other people. Self smart: think and learn by reflecting and thinking inside of self. Word smart: think and learn with words. Picture smart: think and learn with pictures you see or create. Logic smart: think and learn with questions. Music smart: think and learn with rhythms and melodies.[26]

With my little grandson, who is definitely body smart, I regularly speak these sentiments over him: You are smart, you are an adventurer, you make Mimi (that's me) laugh, you are strong. Mommy loves you, Daddy loves you, Grammy loves you, Papa loves you, Mimi loves you. And . . . Jesus loves *you*!

Do you recall the powerful scene in the movie, *The Help*, where the maid reminds the little girl in her charge, "You is kind, you is smart, you is important"?[27] Our kids need to know they are loved and loveable, capable, and purposeful. They view and define themselves by the way we see them and speak about them and to them. How they see themselves plays a huge role in how they tackle hard times.

Dream Squelcher

How we view our kids' and our own personal struggles is critical. We can be helpful or hurtful.

"This too shall pass." "It's just a phase." "They are only little once."

These comments may be true; however, in the moment they are deflating. To our kids we may offhandedly say, "Oh, well that won't matter once you get to college." Or "She wasn't a good friend anyway."

Perspective during hard things, is hard. If we can train our kiddos to think a bit out of the box during less stressful times, they will be more able to utilize the hopeful tool of perspective during challenging moments.

If we approach life being solution focused rather than problem fixated or view life through a realistic positive filter instead of a negative lens, our kids will have a more hopeful model to emulate.

A caution regarding excessive positivity needs to be added here. Training in perspective needs to occur prior to difficult times rather than amid them. In our well-intended efforts to encourage our kids and quickly move them through the feelings of discouragement or disappointment we may create more hopelessness than hopefulness.

Attempts to silence the sad or angry emotions because they make us uncomfortable are misguided. In our discomfort, we want our kids to fast forward through the hurt and feel better. Yet, we must avoid squelching their emotional experience or plastering positive platitudes over the pain.

An optimistic approach taken at the extreme minimizes, denies, discounts, and invalidates difficulties. Insensitive comments masked as feel-good type comments sound like this: "Other people are going through worse." "Look at all you have. How can you feel like that?" "You'll get through it. You are so lucky, you ought to be grateful." "Things will be better in the future." "Everything will work out in the end." "What doesn't kill you makes you stronger."

These comments appear encouraging, helpful, and motivational. Rather they are hurtful and harmful. They disregard the individual's suffering and struggle. Shame and guilt are heaped on an already beaten down person. This may cause that person to isolate and withdraw because they feel misunderstood, unheard, and weak.

When someone feels overwhelmed by life's circumstances, they do not have the strength in that moment to move forward. Repression and emotional stuffing become the coping mechanisms. This adds to the anxiety or depression your loved one may be feeling.

"It doesn't help me to hear, 'Just get up and get going.' I know I need to do that. What I need is the why, 'It usually makes you feel better if . . .' or "You have told me it helps if . . .' 'You have told me it helps to do a small thing like get up or sit on the couch with your boys.'" —Janelle

Perspective has the potential to be helpful if the recipient is ready to receive it. Use this tactic sparingly so that the one suffering does not feel his concern or situation has been discounted or marginalized. Before offering up another perspective, ask, "Are you interested in hearing another perspective?" Then honor the response; if the answer is no, respect that. "OK. Let me know when and if you would like to hear it."

When the suffering person trusts us enough to share their pain, let's allow them the freedom to fully experience and express the anger or sadness that accompanies their situation. Perhaps all that person needs is to vent before moving forward. Allowing them to talk it out may be the medicine needed to gain strength to address the problem.

Helpful hope has a chance to settle in when the person suffering feels listened to, loved, and understood. Allow the feelings to take their natural course. Provide space and time for this process so healing can begin.

Instead of tossing out some toxic positivity, be quiet. We do not have to offer advice. We can listen and reflect, "That sounds hard." "I'm sorry to hear you are going through this." "I can hear the grief in your voice." Offer comfort and compassion. Validate and acknowledge the feeling, "I can see why you feel angry." Or "It's OK not to be OK." Let them know you care, "I'm here for you." Offer assistance, "How can I help?" or "What do you need right now?"

These comments invite conversation. It is good for your kids to fully experience their emotion; it is an emotionally healthy thing to do. We do not want them to fear feelings of anger or hurt. Our kids need to be able to navigate those emotions in a healthy way.

Effective Perspective Training

The best way to train ourselves and our kids to see things out of the box, or to have a heavenly perspective, is to begin to look at positives from an additional perspective.

It can be as simple as, "Thank you, Jesus, for this beautiful sunrise. You could have made it in black and white. But you chose to make it in these vibrant colors for us to enjoy."

Perspective training is intricately linked to regular expressions of gratefulness and thankfulness. I believe it is also connected to empathy and the ability to put ourselves in another's shoes.

When empathy and gratefulness become a part of who we are, we more easily make the paradigm shift to a different perspective. Our outlook on life will be more positive and difficulties appear more like a big hill than an impossible mountain.

Emotional Bypassing

Step by step we climb that hill. Courtney is a person who does not skip steps. She knows she needs to hit each platform before moving onto the next.

"Dad, I do not skip steps." The directions lay folded next to Tom as he put the basketball stand together. Courtney was observing his process.

Our kids purchased a basketball hoop with money they earned from contributing to and helping at our family garage sale. As with most equipment, the box of the basketball hoop contained the dreaded words, "Assembly required."

The corners of his mouth turned up and he unfolded the instructions. He decided it was best to model direction reading—and making certain, like Courtney, he was not going to skip a step.

Tom's experience plus the desire to complete the task quickly contributed to his initial disregard for the assembly instructions. Emotional bypassing is skipping steps. Moms and dads have the experience and know what it takes to alter things to make it better. We want our kids to move to the upper portion of their brain to solve or deal with the problem rather than feel the momentary emotion. Being a witness to our kids' sadness is uncomfortable. We may want to skip that step. We may say emotionally disregarding, discounting, shaming, or dismissive words like: "Just look on the bright side." "Let it go." "Forget about it." "Get over it." "This is not worth crying about."

Our kids need to cope with disappointment. If they have trouble dealing with the hard things in life, negative behaviors will be their coping mechanisms.

"Disappointment is a big trigger for my husband. It causes him to withdraw and give up. He cheated on me for a second time due to disappointment." —Janelle

Allow the emotion. Let the tears flow, they release a stress hormone. Maybe that's why exhaustion and peace follow a good cry.

If we do not allow the expression of emotion and move past it too quickly, soon our kids will learn to wear a mask and pretend all is well. They will pick up on the fact their pain is not something we want to hear about. Those emotions will be stuffed until they can no longer stay hidden.

"The emotions I stuffed away built up. It gradually became harder to act OK when I knew I wasn't. Crying a few times a week turned into a nightly occurrence. And I am not talkin' the cute little sniffling type of crying, but full body sobbing, where your eyes swell up as though an entire colony of bees decided to dive-bomb your face, kind of cry.

"As much as I despised those moments, soon I longed for them. The days where I could not control my sadness or anger would become a luxury, as I would have days where I would feel nothing at all. I thought to myself, 'If I won the lottery today, or found out I had a terminal illness, I would feel the exact same,' a complete absence of emotion or care for anything. These days terrified me the most." —Kendra

It is so hard to read Kendra's reflection about her dark days. During those days her normally cheerful voice was flat, void of emotion. This caused me great concern. Her easy laugh was no longer joining our phone conversations. The four-hour distance between us felt like millions of miles. I prayed like crazy when she told me she was taking short road trips by herself. "God protect Kendra. Comfort her in her sadness."

"Kendra, call me when you get to your destination."

Sometimes she would call. Sometimes she would not answer mine.

I felt helpless. She felt hopeless.

Learn from my mistakes; before your kiddo gets into this deep dark place, make time to sit with your loved one in the hard place. After a bit, help your child move to the thinking part of the brain so the issue can be resolved. Be aware that skipping the emotional processing hinders any learning that could occur or wisdom that could be gained while in the suffering.

My Bad

When I coach parents of adult children, sometimes I hear how those children recount pain and hurt from childhood, pain tied to the parents. We all have wounds from growing up. Kids are not perfect; parents are not perfect. We handle some things well, other things not so well.

Most moms and dads do the best they can and want the best for their children. Life stresses, misguided parenting practices, exhaustion, personal mental health, and unawareness can all contribute to unintended suffering.

That suffering, if it has been deep and consistent, needs to be addressed. Even if there has been a misunderstanding, it is important to respectfully listen. This can be difficult if the child is highly emotional and slinging accusations at the parent.

Here are some ideas to move past the hurt to healing.

1. Be ready to listen and affirm them for speaking up. This is not the time to interrupt, clarify, defend, or question. "I'm so thankful you trust me enough to tell me. You are very brave. I'm listening." This will help take the high emotional responses down a few notches. It will help your child and change something in you.
2. Expect respect. It is possible emotions may run so hot that a conversation cannot be had without name calling or yelling. This type of talk will never be productive. "I want to hear you; I'm distracted by the tone and I find it hard to receive your message."
3. Avoid mirroring their emotions. Remember your goal is relationship healing.
4. Own your stuff. Take responsibility for your mistakes. Do not try and even the score by tossing out their missteps. Apologize and ask for forgiveness. "I'm glad you told me this. I did not intend to hurt you. I am so sorry. I would do things differently today."

5. Acknowledge their pain. This moment is not about how *you* feel. "I see that was hurtful. I'm glad you are telling me this." Avoid saying, "I'm sorry *if* that hurt you." Using the word *if* is an apology loophole; it shrugs off responsibility or culpability. Or avoid using the offensive tactic of turning things around, making the issue about their reaction or character, "You are being a drama queen." Do not accuse them of being overly sensitive. If you want healing to occur, avoid deflection, and stop self-protection types of reactions.

6. Ask for permission to respond. "I'd like to share my perspective and memory of this so we can work through this together." Do not interrupt, justify, blame, or shame. Stick to the facts, not the feelings. If your child says no to your request to respond, be OK with that, "Perhaps we could pick another time to revisit this."

7. Look forward. Ask how you can make restitution or what you can do to make things better going forward. Keep in mind, this conversation is about them and their pain. It is not the time to make it all about you, "Oh, I was the worst mom ever. I never did anything right."

8. Be humble, respectful, loving, and forgiving. It is possible the same issue will resurface if your child wants to continue to punish you. This response will help if that is the case: "I was not a perfect mom. If I could go back and do it differently I would. I have asked God to forgive me. He has. I have asked you to forgive me. And I have forgiven myself." This will put a stop to the adult child who continually wants to play the guilt-and-blame game to increase their perceived sense of power.

Hope Busters
Comparison.
Competition.
Conditional love.

Hope Builders
Identify your child's smarts. Remind them some smarts have not yet been awakened.
Allow your kids freedom to experience and express sadness, fear, or anger.
Acknowledge your child's feelings.

Hopeful Truths
The nurture parents provide matters.
Our words can build up or tear down.
Thankfulness and gratefulness squelch envy.

Prayer

Father, thank You that You don't compare me to others. Thank You that You don't expect perfection from me or my kids. You desire redemption. Help me, help my children, rise up to be the people You created us to be. Amen.

> He will wipe every tear from their eyes. There will be no more death or mourning or crying or pain, for the old order of things has passed away.
> —Revelation 21:4

Chapter 5

THE WAR WITHIN

The one who trusts in him will never be put to shame.

—1 Peter 2:6

Adele kept her secret for ten years. Only one friend knew it, that was the friend she had chosen to be the driver.

"My secret remained a secret for ten years, except for one friend. And that friend knew the secret because my eighteen-year-old self needed a ride to the abortion clinic. That clinic was carefully chosen so my secret would not be uncovered." The clinic was four hours from Adele's home.

"Really, how could I tell any of my other friends? They all had vowed to remain virgins; they would never understand how I let my guard down on prom night."

Adele kept her pregnancy hidden from the baby's father, friends, and family. Years later, she lied to her doctors and her husband about the number of pregnancies she had. Adele, a good person, made a choice that ate her alive for ten years. She thought, I deserve the guilt that I carry. After all, I murdered my baby.

Guilt, shame, remorse, fear of rejection were her constant companions. She believed that she needed to carry the weight of the guilt because she was solely responsible for her actions. She deserved misery. As the years passed, Adele and her husband had two children.

"I decided I needed to make up for the abortion by being the perfect mom with two perfect kids. The more driven I was to be perfect, the more anger simmered beneath the surface." She was angry with her former boyfriend, with her imperfect children and flawed husband. She was angry with the abortion clinic.

"Guilt was steering the ship. Guilt is a terrible captain," Adele told me. Hope eluded her because she was unable to embrace grace. She knew she was saved yet she did not know about God's unconditional love and didn't understand Jesus' grace.

"Because I had been so bad, I needed to be, had to be, so good. Good works were my payment, the penance for aborting my child. I was convinced my works would square things with God."[28]

Wear the Mask

Adele wore her mask, the mask of the perfect person doing perfect things. Beneath the facade was a hurting person, one who feared rejection and carried a heavy load of remorse. She thought her salvation was in her works. She believed her self-preservation was in her public presentation.

Kendra also donned her mask, a mask of happiness. She believed being a happy person all the time was who she had to be, no matter what.

People are drawn to Kendra. She is the light in the room. Her easy laugh, tender heart, interest in others, and quick humor make her someone others desire to be around. This is who she is, but she is multifaceted, not one-dimensional. Somewhere along the way, she thought her role in life was to make others feel good by her happy, carefree disposition. This belief made it difficult to show and share her true emotional struggles.

"I continuously pushed them (emotions of sadness) down and portrayed myself as how I envisioned everyone had viewed me before, a happy-go-lucky girl."—Kendra

Kendra is not alone in her attempt to mask her feelings. Many people who struggle with depression or anxiety hide their feelings. They do not want to make others uncomfortable; to admit something is wrong is embarrassing. "No one will understand. People will think I'm crazy," are common thoughts.

Fake Book

"It seems there is so much pressure to always be happy. Social media often makes it seem that everyone is just fantastic, and no one is struggling. Because let's get real, how many people actually post things about their bad days or hard times? Know that even if it looks like you are the only person that feels the way you do, you're not. When I look at pictures I posted while I was contemplating suicide daily, I looked so happy. You can't always trust what others choose to show." —Kendra

The happy expectation prevents those struggling from getting help. It feeds the belief that something must be wrong with you because everyone appears good and you are not. Kids conclude, "Everyone else is happy all the time. What is wrong with me?"

Dr. Kathy Koch, in her book *Screens and Teens,* talks about this very phenomenon. She describes five lies that technology overtly or covertly speaks to our young people. Lie number two is, "I deserve to be happy all the time."[29] Many young people perceive that happiness is the baseline feeling. It is one of four main emotions with anger, sadness, and fear being the other three. Our kiddos need life experience in all four areas, so they are able to successfully do life. Parents sheltering their kids from difficulty and running disappointment interference contributes to the happy lie, as does social media.

It seems everyone wants everybody else to think their life is problem-free, exciting, and happy. Just as they post their best, they forget others are doing the very same thing. Perfect posts and filtered photos present a false reflection of someone's life. Social media pictures are the highlight reels in someone's life. Young adults view the images and believe no one else feels sad, lonely, or discouraged. They falsely believe they are the only one smiling fake smiles and everyone else is living the large Instagram perfect life.

This dynamic causes shame which creates a situation where depression goes underground. Psychologists call this, The Duck Syndrome.[30] Envision a duck seemingly skimming effortlessly through the water while beneath the surface their little webbed feet are frantically working to keep them afloat and moving.

Repeated and regular exposure to idealized photos can elicit envy and may trigger depression in some. The one-dimensional images do not represent real life.

"If your fear is loss of pride or image, try to recognize that the image you are attempting to uphold may not be true. And in the end, if protecting that fake image is the most important thing, and you succumb to the terrible whispers that haunt you . . . how will that idea of you hold up? Well . . . it won't. And let me be the first to say that people (at least the right ones) love honesty, humbleness, and transparency. Those qualities show more character and poise than any perfectly happy and calculated Instagram ever could. Helping yourself by opening up is building a good image of you, not taking it away." —Kendra

I wish I had the social media conversation with each of my kids before they began dabbling in it. Kendra may have not struggled as much if we had an honest conversation about the reality of the fakeness of social media. I didn't help her align her expectations with real life; people are not always happy and they do go through struggles. I wish I had taken her emotional temperature pre-suicidal ideation. I believe it would have helped her if I had regularly asked, "Kendra, how are you doing—today?" She needed to know, it is OK if she is not happy all the time and she was not alone in this.

Tender Hearts

"It's not a secret that I am a fairly sensitive person. My emotions are big and loud, whether it be happiness, anger, or sadness. I feel very intensely and tend to outwardly portray those feelings. This type of personality can be a blessing in many ways, but it can also be a curse. I believe I have a larger capacity for love and appreciation than many, but on the flip side, my capacity to hurt runs deeper than most." —Kendra

Our strengths can also be our weaknesses. In Kendra's case the tenderness and sensitivity she possesses and extends to others, turned internal. Her vision of other's reality and her own was distorted.

Her vision needed correction. Kendra would concur, "Without the right tools and knowledge on how to manage these feelings, they can easily take full control of me."

Kendra hits the nail on the head. Coping skills are necessary when that sensitive spirit embraces and clings to negative thoughts and feelings. Those thoughts are no longer filtered through reality. Kendra describes this as, "A vicious virus that engulfed my heart and mind." Introverts, highly sensitive people, or empaths tend to turn inward. They are more susceptible to feelings of helplessness and hopelessness.

People who are empaths or highly sensitive individuals have their sensitivity superpowers turn against them. They move from disappointment to despair to depression. Or worry to fear to anxiety.

Here are some assessment questions to help determine if your child is a highly sensitive person (HSP).

1. Does your child absorb the feelings of others? This individual feels another's pain as if it was their own. They may say, "My heart aches for you."
2. Do timed quizzes or tests cause anxiety? The child may not only fret but freeze, rendering them unable to do the test. "All I could think about was the clock ticking away. It gave me a stomachache."
3. Does your child withdraw when overstimulated? If the environment becomes too loud, too intense, the child may run off. "This is too much. It's too loud. I'm getting a headache."
4. Does your child have an exaggerated startle reflex? This child is hypervigilant and jumps sky high when surprised or frightened. "You scared me to death!"
5. Is your child unable to deal with conflict? Highly sensitive kids pick up on and react to negative vibes and have difficulty handling disagreement. "Are you mad? You seem mad."
6. Does your child overthink decisions? Decisions are problematic for the HSP. They continually change their

minds and are unable to move forward. "I'm afraid if I do this, then that might happen."

7. Does your child have a highly active imagination? Many HSP kids have a busy internal thought life. They may have an imaginary friend or regularly engage in make-believe play.

8. Is change or transition especially difficult and stress inducing? The thought of change can cause the highly sensitive kid to have a meltdown.

9. Does criticism totally crush your child's spirit? Criticism is devastating to the highly sensitive person. They may exclaim, "Everything I do is wrong."

10. Is your child very insightful and perceptive? Highly sensitive kids are observant and pick up on nuances and social cues that most others miss. "Did you see how upset he got after she left?"

Those cumulative sensitive feelings can be the catalyst for anxiety or depression if a way to manage them is not learned. Highly sensitive kids need coping mechanisms to deal with sensory overload.

Destructive Doubt

Sensory overload is overwhelming and causes procrastination and overthinking. We speak life when we help our kids have a proper perspective of their circumstances and who they are-- their gifts, talents, and weaknesses. A lack of confidence is not an indicator of a lack of ability or love-ableness.

Procrastination and doubt arise from depleted confidence. Lack of confidence is a broken record; it ruminates and perseverates. Potential or present problems are the things on which we fixate rather than the solution. Like a broken record, the negative thoughts spin and spin and get stuck on the same sorry lyrics: It is all my fault, this will ruin my entire life, I will feel like this forever.

Have you heard your kids express at least one of those hopeless statements? I'm guessing you have. You may have even spoken them yourself. Rather than feed into this type of negative pattern it is up to parents to help their children find hope in the situation by changing the chorus.

A healthy reflection and assessment of the situation is called for, not rumination. Guide your kids so they can refocus on a solution rather than fixate on the concern. This can be done through questions and statements.

Acknowledge their feelings, then guide them toward figuring out a solution. To build confidence, it is important for the young person to come up with the ideas. Not only do we want our kids to know we understand by acknowledging their feelings, but we also want them to participate in the solution to the problem. If they are unable to be a part of the solution, they will begin to feel a sense of helplessness which could lead to hopelessness. They need to know they can do hard things.

"I see you feel responsible. What can you do to make it better?"

Another technique for our kids to learn is to help them see interactions objectively rather than subjectively. Subjective observation assumes an action, thought, or feeling is directly related to the speaker, "She didn't pick up the phone because she hates me."

Objective statements contain only facts, "She didn't answer the phone." There are no judgments, conclusion, or presuppositions. It is simply a statement of truth.

A third way to get out of the broken record mindset is to avoid the adverbs *always* and *never*. Those two words are total hope suckers. There is no room for hope if something will always be the same and never change.

There are things that are out of one's control. *Outies* do not change. Outies need to be separated from *innies*; those things that we can control. When our kids learn how to recognize the innies from the outies, they will feel empowered to act or to learn to let it go and trust God.

Rejection Stings

One of the outies I cannot control is how others feel about me. I like to be liked. I want to be included. (Brace yourself because this can really knock me down.) Not everyone likes me. I am not always included. This is reality. I hate it but it is one I need to accept.

Recently, my oldest child felt the sting of rejection. We had a conversation about trusted and loyal relationships. I drew three concentric circles. The center circle held her closest and most trusted relationships: her parents, siblings, a mentor, and one very dear friend. The next circle represented committed and more casual relationships like extended family members. The largest circle held acquaintances; this included everyone else plus social media connections. We discussed what qualifies as a confidant and a true friend: mutual sharing of hearts, the desire to resolve interpersonal conflict in a constructive way, and commitment to time spent together.

Rejection and betrayal will be a part of our kids' stories. We know it is true. We have experienced it. Jesus experienced it. Betrayal and exclusion hurt. Rejection brings on feelings of anger, anxiety, depression, sadness, and jealousy.

"Rejection is hard no matter who you are or what phase of life you're in. It stings to feel less than desirable or unwanted. But in the midst of intense depression, the smallest thing could make me feel rejected. I had no reserves to 'brush things off' or to recognize when things weren't 'a big deal.' Not being invited to a dinner with my roommates, an acquaintance not smiling at me as we crossed paths, a seemingly judging look from a stranger; honestly, any interaction that didn't go perfectly was fair game. In my eyes, everything reflected back on me in some negative way. I thought, 'What is wrong with me that made other people treat me this way?' And each moment compounded onto one another, they were not singular events, but continuing proof that I deserved to feel lonely and I wasn't enough." —Kendra

It is tough for me to comprehend that my loving daughter felt like this. The mom in me feels anger (*big anger*) at people who have hurt my kid. I am like Kendra; I am sensitive to people's reactions or lack of reaction. I personalize the moment. I notice other people's responses and attach their behavior to how they view me. When a person is in a vulnerable emotional state this is intensified.

I am learning to separate my feelings from the real experience. Looking at the situation from an objective perspective can *sometimes* be helpful. However, another perspective may not fully heal the pain. My husband and I were not included in a big event. We took a moment to process the exclusion by looking at it from the other person's perspective. That helped a bit.

It was understandable why we were not invited; it was a gathering we would have felt uncomfortable attending. Those doing the inviting were confident we would not attend. Yet, we were hurt a conversation about this did not occur prior to the invites being sent out. Logically it made sense not to receive an invitation. It was the lack of communication that was confusing and hurtful.

For us—well, maybe more for me—I needed to embrace grace and grant forgiveness in this mess. This was not something to verbalize but something to internalize—a private response to a hurtful occurrence. The recipients of my forgiveness would not have felt as if they needed it. They were operating from a logical point of view. My head understood this. Yet my heart needed to be right before God and sensitive to the other party's point of view. To go forward with relationship reconciliation, which requires two people, my hurt feelings needed to be tenderized with grace. When I could respond from a grace place my words and actions could start the mending and healing process.

I chose to believe this exclusion was not intended to hurt us. I could have concluded the opposite. But why would I? I know they love me. Why not assume the best, especially if the relationship is precious to me?

I am learning to ask questions to understand rather than accuse and think the worst. A helpful strategy is to state what I know to be true about the person who has hurt me. I know this person loves me. I know this person is kind and not mean spirited. I know this person operates out of logic, not emotion.

Following a clarifying conversation that centered on the things we both care about, we were both OK. We understood each point of view and accepted that we see things slightly differently. The conversation gave us the ability to move past the situation to the solution.

It is critical to find common ground, then step forward in grace rather than camp on the pain. If you want to move forward, focus on the solution and embrace grace.

Determining one's goal and expressing the hoped-for outcome keeps the conversation solution focused. If my reason to connect had been to focus on my pain of rejection, we would have had an entirely different conversation with a totally different outcome. Accusations and justifications only cause division. My goal was to reach an understanding so we could take positive steps forward. Together we decided to improve the relationship through more open and frequent communication. I am thankful we talked, listened, and cleared up some misunderstandings. And yes, going forward our relationship has been strengthened and become closer.

Back Talk

Post rejection, resist the urge to engage in negative self-talk. Change up the unhealthy self-talk to positive messages. Remember who God created you to be. Thank Him for the skills and talents and Godly qualities He has given you.

Thanking God for your good qualities and natural abilities is an uncomfortable exercise.

One of my clients continually feels the pain of rejection from her adult daughter.

"Gina, write down all the positive traits God has given you. Then speak those traits to your reflection in the mirror."

"This is a God boast, not a Gina brag. Boast in Him the wonderful qualities He blessed you with."

This activity caused discomfort. Gina had trouble coming up with descriptive adjectives. I assisted her: kind, compassionate, tender hearted. Then I encouraged her to have her husband add to the list.

Rejection hurts. Gratitude in how God has created us can bring some healing to that wound. This tactic can be used with your children when they are hurting.

Stabbing Pain

Rejection from a family member cuts deep.

"My dad is really hard on certain grandkids. Hudson is one of his targets. In front of my son, I confronted and corrected my father. That moment was powerful for my son. It was a turning point for him." —Sarah

Parents, we can offer hope when we acknowledge our kids' feelings rather than ignore them. We can be their protector and advocate. Rejection hurts.

Even if it creates discomfort in you, be OK with a time of grieving over rejection. Let the tears roll. Allow space for your child's emotional expression so the hurt can be healed.

"My sixteen-year-old son Landon struggles to make friends. His peers pick on him. He even had a situation when he was in seventh grade and some of his wrestling teammates threatened to kill him and our family because he did not wear a particular T-shirt to school. He was so afraid that these kids would come to our home and hurt us. At the same time a girl in his P.E. class was consistently kidney punching him. Recently he asked three different girls to prom. They all turned him down. One of the girls made a big scene after he asked her. There were years he would cry every day before school. 'I don't want to go to school, I'd rather be dead. Everyone hates me and makes fun of me.' He gets migraines often and becomes sick to his stomach."

Lucinda is ready and available to listen to her son, Landon. She has sought help from the school regarding the bullying, and from other experts. Like Lucinda, when your kiddos are ready to talk, be available to listen and be their best advocate. God can use parents and others to reduce the impact of rejection.

Rejection may feel devastating, but it does not have to be debilitating.

"If your fear is rejection, realize that those who reject you in this time of need are not worth holding on to (at least for now). Rejection can be a gift because, in the end, it shows you who will be there for you in your time of need. The perspective I had on my social circle changed drastically once my issues came to the surface. At first, it can be a hard pill to swallow, but later on, becomes a breath of fresh air to have that knowledge." —Kendra

Have the Talk

Talking about the issue and airing your feelings can be therapeutic. This does not replace speaking directly to the one who caused the pain. In many cases, it is appropriate to directly talk with the person who hurt you. The conversation could look like this:

Gently ask, "Why did this happen? I wish I would have been included." Do not make the assumption they are to blame for leaving you out.

"I felt sad when all you guys went hiking last Saturday and didn't include me. I realize I worked Friday night, but I was totally up for hanging out Saturday. I figured out I was not included when another friend filled me in on your hike. Was there a reason you didn't think to include me?"

Observe the person's response, explanation, and behavior going forward. This will tell you a lot. It is possible they may be surprised you felt left out. They may have made an assumption or a choice based on what they knew. If it was intentional that will be evident in time.

Now is the time to address any misconceptions or assumptions and state your hope going forward. Decide upon your goal for the conversation. If your goal is to heap a load of guilt on someone, the conversation will create further division and the wound gap will grow. If the goal is to restore and repair the relationship, a grace-filled attitude needs to bathe the conversation.

If rejection continues despite your efforts, it is time to release the relationship. Look for people who can be counted on, who are kind, trustworthy, who respect and care about you. Letting go and reaching for new friendships is a hard step but sticking around and continually being kicked is worse.

Hope Busters
Overly sensitive.
Overthinking.
Overly critical.

Hope Builders
Discuss the reality of the fakeness of social media.
Regularly ask your child, "How are you doing—today?"
Acknowledge their feelings, guide them toward figuring out a solution, "I see you feel responsible. What can you do to make it better?"

Hopeful Truths
Not everyone is happy all the time, no matter what their social media looks like.
It is OK not to be happy all the time.
Feelings are not facts. Feelings are temporary.

Prayer

Father, remove my guilt and replace it with Your grace. Take my shame and give me confidence in Your salvation. Remove the veil so I can see life has challenging times for all, even those who look like life is perfect. Let me be OK even when life is not OK. Amen.

> Shame . . . is not guilt. Shame is a focus on self. Guilt is a focus on behavior. Shame is "I *am* bad"; guilt is "I *did* something bad."[31]
>
> —Brené Brown

Chapter 6

FAITH FACTOR

Cast all your anxiety on him because he cares for you.

—1 Peter 5:7

Picture this, the Grand Canyon filled with water. That's Lake Powell. The lake is 561 feet deep, there are over 2,000 miles of shoreline, and it is over 186 miles long. The lake lies in the lap of Arizona and Utah.

We began our family adventure at the Bullfrog Marina. There we boarded our houseboat and got a speedboat. We were able to explore the lake and all its hidden bays, each big enough to be a lake of its own.

We came upon a spot where some brave (or crazy) souls were jumping off the red rock cliffs into the 80-degree water. From the safety of our speed boat, this looked like fun. (As I write this my hands have begun to sweat.) We docked our boat, meaning we pulled it up on a flat space on shore, with the expectation the rising waves would not sweep the boat away.

The kids clamored out of the boat and started to climb the smooth and slippery red rocks. Tom and I chased after them. As we climbed up, I realized from this perspective, the distance that separated the lake from the jumping point was a whole lot higher than I expected.

"No one is jumping off into the water! Look how the waves are crashing against the rocks. Do you guys hear me? No one, I said no one, is jumping off." They grumbled and complied.

"Mom's freaking out. We can't jump off."

Like a herd of mountain goats, they continued to climb and explore, with my husband smack dab in the middle of the herd. Me, I sat frozen on the rock, thinking, "I'm going to slip right off, fall a bazillion feet into that tumultuous water, and get tossed against the rocks like a ragdoll. If the fall does not kill me, the waves and rocks will." My heart was beating out of my chest, my hands a sweaty mess. My thoughts centered on, "Someone is going to die." Was I the only one who could discern how dangerous this was?

The five made it back to the boat. "Come on, Mom, we want to go." They were oblivious to the fear that gripped me. I crab-walked along the rocks. There was no way I was standing up. I prayed without ceasing. Every little hand plant and footstep was a faith feat and a God trust. I made it back to the boat by sliding my bottom across the smooth rock.

That same fear of heights still claims my mind and body. I know my faith in the Lord is strong. I understand my fear is irrational. It does not matter. I am still afraid of heights.

Faith Factor

I have a faith and a fear of heights. I relate to Jennifer Vail when she says, "I can have anxiety and still love Jesus."[32] Anxiety does not define her faith. Jennifer suffers with anxiety and has most of her life. "I wake up most mornings struggling to breathe because my body is so seized with panic."[33]

Jennifer is a believer who loves Jesus with her whole heart, mind, and soul. She knows God is good. She prays, studies Scripture, and worships. And she experiences anxiety daily.

Many people struggle with anxiety like Jennifer. There are a multitude of reasons why someone experiences depression, anxiety, loneliness, or fear. Heredity, trauma, stress, and perfectionism are among the reasons folks struggle.

There are those who believe mental illness is the result of an immature faith. Not so; all we need to do is read Psalms, Ruth, Lamentations, or the book of Job and hear the cries of anguish contained in these books. Anxiety, depression, loneliness, and fear were experienced by our biblical heroes.

Job's quote in Job 7:15, "I prefer strangling and death, rather than this body of mine," or David's lament in Psalm 6:3–6,

> My soul is in deep anguish.
>> How long, LORD, how long?
> Turn, LORD, and deliver me;
>> save me because of your unfailing love.
> Among the dead no one proclaims your name.
>> Who praises you from the grave?
> I am worn out from my groaning.
> All night long I flood my bed with weeping
>> and drench my couch with tears.

And Naomi in the book of Ruth says, "'Don't call me Naomi,' she told them. 'Call me Mara, because the Almighty has made my life very bitter'" (1:20). These verses speak of the struggles Job, David, and Naomi experienced.

Mental illness is not reserved for people with a lack of faith or unconfessed sin. Mental illness, like physical illness, affects all: believers, strong believers, seekers, and non-believers. A believer is not immunized from suffering.

Here are some truths Jennifer relays about anxiety. It is not: a defiance of God, a lack of faith, a statement of trust or lack of trust, always cured with fervent prayers, or simply worry. It is a chemical reaction, a condition. And . . . you can have anxiety and still love Jesus.[34]

Many believers who suffer from anxiety feel ashamed. Often believers will not share their fears because their faith is questioned. They are reluctant to ask for help for fear of being viewed as a person who cannot trust God.

Some believers wonder if a person loves Jesus why can't they trust Him with their anxiety? Jennifer answers this way, "The same way the diabetic can. The same way the anemic can. The same way the arthritic, the cancer-stricken, the blind, the infertile, the sick, and the well can. Because this condition is not a result of lack of faith, and having more faith cannot alone heal it."[35]

Jennifer acknowledges God can heal and deliver. Even if this side of heaven He does not take away anxiety, she and other sufferers are no less Christian.

As Jennifer says, "I have a medical condition and a Savior, and there is nothing in our Bible that tells me I can't."[36]

My Lake Powell experience was a tiny taste of the meal she has daily. Even though I cannot fully grasp the daily struggle anxiety brings, I do have empathy for it. Faith helps you through the fear, one crab-walk step at a time. Faith moves you toward your goal, despite your fear. Victory comes in small steps.

Subtract the voice that claims if they believed hard enough, long enough, deep enough, anxiety or fear would disappear. This attitude piles shame upon a person already riddled with it.

Depression, fear, loneliness, and anxiety are like a thorn in the flesh. Paul begged the Lord to take away his thorn. He prayed three times for the Lord to remove it. No one knows what Paul's thorn was. What we do know is that sometimes God does not remove the thorn (2 Corinthians 12:8).

In 2 Corinthians 12:7 we see where the thorn was embedded. It was in Paul's flesh. This was a huge *aha!* for me; the thorn was in his flesh, not his faith. "Therefore, in order to keep me from becoming conceited, I was given a thorn in my flesh, a messenger of Satan, to torment me."

Even though Paul suffered with his thorn, he remained on his mission to preach the gospel. Those suffering with depression or anxiety or any other thorn can still serve our Lord. Paul did not live a pain-free life. In his suffering he continued to make a difference in the world, then and now!

Not OK Is OK

We look at Paul, Naomi, David, and Job and we conclude being not OK, is OK. When a loved one dies or depression sets in, it is OK not to be OK. These are the times we must be patient with and kind to ourselves. Sometimes we survive rather than thrive.

"It's OK to not be OK. It does not make you selfish or weak, all it means is you need some help and support. And after going through what I have, I realized how strong and capable I am. I never thought I would see the day where I broke free of that heaviness, that suffocation. But *I* did. And if I had been successful in my attempt to take my life, there are so many beautiful experiences I would have missed out on: meeting my first nephew, graduating college, becoming a nurse, and so many friendships and relationships.

"I may not be able to fully empathize with your situation, and probably can't even fathom some of the trials you are facing: abuse, neglect, financial struggles, heartbreak, health issues, death of loved ones, drugs, the list could go on and on. But no matter the reason for your sadness, or even if there is no true reason at all, I know that you have the tools inside you and around you to not only fight this battle, but to win it." —Kendra

("I never thought I would see the day where I broke free of that heaviness, that suffocation. But *I* did." These two sentences are my favorite lines in this book. Praise God.)

Make It Stop

The pain those struggling with deep depression or anxiety experience is beyond what most people can understand.

"It is a huge misconception, in my mind, that reading the Bible or hearing a Scripture verse will completely alter another's suicidal ideation. Those who attempt or contemplate suicide have already run out of their own ability to understand their worth, no matter how many times they are told. Action is what matters.

"Having someone *show* their love by physically being present and actively being love for me is what made a difference." —Kendra

Suicide is not that people want to die, it is that they don't want to live.

Words that add to the anguish of those who have loved ones who have attempted or completed suicide are:

Statement	Truth
"That is an unforgivable sin."	Not true. We are not judged by the last thing we did.
"That is the most selfish thing someone can do."	Wrong perspective. They are in so much pain their perception of reality is totally off.
"How couldn't you see the signs?"	Unkind and uninformed. Depressed people learn how to compensate for their sadness by putting on a mask.

"My decision-making skills took a total plunge during this time. They fluctuated between haphazard, rash, and extreme. I often felt numb to the world around me and I was hoping in my recklessness, it might spring up some emotion. I spent money I didn't have, I drove down winding mountain roads going over 100 mph, I said things that were rude or out of line. It's painful to look back and realize how I was acting, because when I am mentally healthy, that is so unlike me. I was unbelievably uncomfortable inside myself, with no good explanation, that I think I wanted to experience discomfort outwardly as well . . . because then my sadness or lack of emotion would make sense and have a reason behind it." —Kendra

I cannot even read this. I feel sick to my stomach. How could I not fully grasp her desperation? I knew Kendra wrestled with depression. I was aware she was struggling. I felt concern she was on shaky ground. I had no idea how shaky the ground beneath her was.

Even though I did not know the degree of suffering my child was experiencing, I knew I needed to be with her. I planned to drive to Grand Junction the next day. I thought making plans together for the following day would prevent her from harming herself.

I was wrong. Thankfully God heard my prayers and protected her those twenty-four hours before I arrived. God prevented her attempt from succeeding.

Many who are deadly serious about suicide, tell no one. They make their plans privately.

"My husband and I heard a loud noise, like someone falling. We ran upstairs to our fifteen-year-old daughter Annie's room. She had attempted to hang herself from her ceiling fan. We also learned she was cutting and self-medicating using prescription drugs. We took her to Children's Hospital and then she was transferred to a mental health facility. We didn't even know she was struggling with suicidal thoughts. She seemed like she had it all together. She was on the honor role, a cheerleader, and a very responsible teenager."—Michelle

Michelle and her husband immediately sought help for their child. Depression is a serious mental illness that needs treatment.

"Our youngest daughter also attempted suicide by hanging. She had just been rejected by a boy. Suicide at her high school has become a problem. Thank the Lord she told us so we could get her help. We feel very hopeful because she came to us, she wants to learn how to cope when life is hard, and she wants to get better."—Michelle

Depression is treatable. It takes hard work and the will to get healthy. Those suffering from it cannot just snap out of it. With so much negative social stigma surrounding mental illness, many do not seek help. Untreated depression is the number one cause for suicide. There is no shame in getting help. It is a brave thing to do.

Those suffering from depression and suicidal ideation need to know people care about them. Check in, ask them, "How are you today?" I wish I had asked Kendra, "Have you been crying a lot?" Don't be afraid to ask the hard question, "Are you having thoughts of suicide?" If the answer is yes, follow-up with the unthinkable question of, "Have you made a plan?" Then remove the items they may use to harm themselves. Listen with compassion and be ready to call 911 if you believe they are in immediate danger.

Notice if they are making irrational decisions and acting strangely. Before attempting to take her life, Kendra quit her job, packed up her belongings, and told her roommates she was going to commute four hours to school and back to Morrison on the days of her classes. This extreme behavior was a cry for help.

Even younger kids may cry out for help. "When I die, bury me with my favorite tractor," fourth grader, Mikey, directed his wishes to his mom, Shelby. ADD (Attention Deficit Disorder), a mood disorder, and depression plagued Mikey. When Mikey was out of sorts, his dad would take him for a long hike to get those endorphins going. Mikey is now Mike, a young adult who still has depression and understands the importance of self-care.

New Lonely

Depression, avoidance, anger, grief, disappointment, failure, and exhaustion are some reasons people isolate or withdraw from others. Isolation increases loneliness and loneliness can lead to hopelessness.

Mental and spiritual health are both affected by isolation. Withdrawing, unless it is done for reflection and re-centering, is not a healthy strategy. Choosing to withdraw is an opportunity for the enemy to speak his lies to the person who is shutting down.

There is a new lonely that young people are now experiencing. "Recent research suggests that young people actually feel loneliness more intensely, and more frequently, than any other age group."[37]

Intuitively, we know there is a connection between loneliness and mental health and social media use. Now there is a study to back that up from the University of Pennsylvania. There is a link between social media use and decreased well-being. Psychologist Melissa G. Hunt said, "Here's the bottom line: Using less social media than you normally would leads to significant decreases in both depression and loneliness. These effects are particularly pronounced for folks who were more depressed when they came into the study."[38]

Hunt is not suggesting that young adults should stop using social media, which would be an unrealistic goal. Rather she recommends limiting screen time on social media apps like Facebook, Snapchat, and Instagram.

"I don't scroll for hours. It's those little micro-moments that add up. I began using the screen time app and noticed I was on social media two hours a day. It's crazy how those little moments add up. I'm trying to cut it in half. On the days I'm more successful in reducing social media time, I feel less weighed down, less stressed. The phone is kind of an addiction. It is hard to realize because everyone is on it, doing the same thing. When you try to stop or slow down you realize how much you reach for your phone. It just keeps your mind so busy. In a way, it is a little hard to reduce the time because you don't want to be unaware of what is going on or feel like you are not included." —Kendra

Unmasking Fear

Loneliness, anxiety, and depression are tied closely to fear. My friend Melinda Means intimately knows fear. She penned these words in her blog:

"Autoimmune disease began to attack my body at the age of 27. Over time, even the most 'harmless' foods and substances could produce debilitating pain and inflammation in my body. I was terrified of getting infected by bacteria and viruses because typical prescribed treatments often triggered other symptoms in my already screwed-up system. I feared the 'cure' as much as the infection.

"When my second child was born with cystic fibrosis, my 'germ anxiety' only intensified. Now, I didn't only fear for myself, but for my son. Micah's diagnosis meant that even a simple cold or flu virus could potentially permanently steal precious lung function. When he was a baby and toddler, I washed my hands so often they were cracked and bleeding. I lived in a state of hypervigilance for nearly two decades."[39]

"I remember saying to God, 'I can't do this anymore. This isn't living. You are my only Hope.' And immediately I believe God gave me this thought: 'You can trust the One who died for you.' In that moment, something shifted in me."[40]

Kick Fear to the Curb

Perfect love comes from the One who died for Melinda and for you and me. Scripture says in 1 John 4:18, perfect love casts out fear. Perfect love rids us of the fear of judgement. Perfect love also causes us to rise up and be brave in frightening situations.

Kendra's friend Danae's actions show us what perfect love casting out fear looks like.

Tom and I picked Duncan up from the airport. Kendra, Rain, and Danae were still in Peru. Kendra had been a victim of a robbery. The U.S. Embassy called us the day before to inform us that she needed money to get a temporary passport, which was also stolen, in order to get home. Duncan filled us in on the rest of the details.

"I thought she was dead," Duncan's voice came from the back seat of our car. "A masked gunman had pushed Kendra up against the wall, with the gun aimed at her head. The gun went off and she dropped to the ground." He was describing the last day of the four college students' five-week backpacking trip. I closed my eyes and inhaled deeply as Tom's hands white knuckled the wheel.

Duncan and three girls had two hours left before leaving Peru's lush jungles, deserts, glaciers, and beaches. They had just gone to the grocery store with their Peruvian friend, Diego, so they could whip up a final meal together. As they stepped out of the car, arms filled with groceries and last-minute souvenirs, two men charged them. The men's hands held the guns; cocked and ready to fire.

Confusion filled the moment. "Was this a prank?"

"No, no, no!" Diego shouted as he ran. He knew it wasn't. He understood his car was the prize.

Thinking this was a joke, Kendra and Danae ran after Diego and the two masked men.

The confusion cleared when they observed the men beating and pistol-whipping Diego.

"Hey! Stop it! Leave him alone."

The gunmen's attention was diverted to Kendra and Danae. With Diego's car keys in one hand and a gun in the other the men turned their attention to their next victims.

Wallets, purses, iPhones, and credit cards were next on the list. The bandits went for whatever could be quickly snatched. Anyone slowing them down was an obstacle to be dealt with.

My daughter, frozen with fear, was too slow for them. They pushed her and grabbed her bag. The cord attached to her bag was strong. Adrenaline filled, one of the masked men, yanked the cord, tossed Kendra to the ground and shot his gun. The gun aimed at her head; point blank range.

Kendra dropped. Head ringing, pounding. Sound silenced.

"Ken, get up. Get up. Hurry," Danae cried out.

"I'm shot! Did he shoot off my ear?" Kendra looked up and saw the gun pointed at her, angry eyes glaring through the slits in the mask. "Please . . . no . . ."

Kendra had fallen near the car, the object of the attack. It now doubled as the get-away vehicle. She was preventing them from fleeing. Dazed, she thought he would shoot her again.

A familiar voice broke through. "Get up!"

Danae ran over to Kendra and pulled her up. They escaped to the safety of a Peruvian home. Duncan and Rain did the same. The community, now aware an attack was occurring in their neighborhood, stepped in to help. One young man flung a piece of metal at the car windshield. It connected to its target. Unable to see, the robbers crashed the car, got out, shot again, and ran off.

God protected the five young people from serious injury. Miracle of miracles, Kendra was not shot. God provided people to help.

Danae's perfect love for Kendra cast out any fear. She never left Kendra, even at great risk to herself. Love conquers fear.

Tom and I were anxious to get Kendra home from her Peruvian adventure. After taking only a day to get the necessary paperwork done, the three girls flew out of Lima to Atlanta.

We got a second phone call, "Hey Mom, our flight is overbooked, and we can get free airline tickets if we get on the next flight. Can I give up my tickets?"

Perfect love casts out fear. And perfect love also says, "No." Perfect love wants their kid home after they have been shot at.

God with Us

God fully showed Himself in Peru. Kendra had no money to get a temporary passport, but God put a man in line behind her at the U. S. Embassy, dressed in army fatigues, who gave her in cash the $140.00 U.S. dollars she needed.

"Thank you. What's your name?"

"Israel." God let Kendra know He was with her. My family and friends prayed for God's protection, provision, and for people to step up and help. Diego, stitched up, stepped in to navigate the Peruvian bureaucracy. Kendra's two girlfriends stayed behind, missing their flight, so she would not be alone. It only took one day to accomplish what should have taken at least two.

In the dark moments, the ones marked by depression, anxiety, or fear, God is with us and He wants us to know. "So do not fear, for I am with you; do not be dismayed, for I am your God. I will strengthen you and help you; I will uphold you with my righteous right hand" (Isaiah 41:10).

Hope Busters
Perpetual social media use.
Perfectionism.
Persistent pain.

Hopeful Truths
Biblical heroes suffered from fear, anxiety, and depression.
Anxiety, depression, and fear are not a lack of faith.
God is with us.

Hope Builders
Practice identifying real fear and false fear. Imagined fear often begins with, "What if."
Remember and document the ways God has shown up in difficult times.
Pray Joshua 1:9, "Lord make (my child) strong and courageous. Do not let (child's name) be fearful or discouraged because (name) knows You will be with (name) wherever he/she goes."

Prayer

Lord God, help me to have clear vision. Remove the veil from my eyes so I am able to see when my child is struggling. Give me courage to ask the hard questions. Stop words or sentiments that stir guilt or shame. Provide wisdom so I can guide my child as he or she seeks help. Amen.

> Fear and trembling have beset me;
> horror has overwhelmed me.
> —Psalm 55:5

Chapter 7

FAMILY
RESEMBLANCE

So God created mankind in his own image, in the image of God he created them; male and female he created them.

—Genesis 1:27

It was a bit puzzling. Michael, my first-grade student, turned in his color-by-number assignment. The colors and numbers did not match. I wondered if he was having trouble reading the names of the colors on the paper.

"Hey Michael, could you read the names of the colors on your worksheet to me?"

"Sure Mrs. W." He obliged. He read red, green, blue, yellow, purple. He was spot on, no issue with decoding words.

I removed my teacher hat and donned my detective cap. Perhaps he didn't know his colors. "Can you show me the blue crayon?" We went through all the colors; he got stuck on red and green.

This was my first experience with a color-blind student. The next item on the agenda was to see the school nurse and confirm my suspicions. She had a booklet that identified color deficiency called the Ishihara Color Vision Test. Each page contained one circle with a pattern made up of many dots of various sizes, different colors, and brightness.

The dots are arranged in a way that a person with typical color vision will be able to see a single-digit or two-digit number within the circle. A color-blind person will not be able to see the number or may see a different number than the one a person with normal color vision will see.

The nurse did a quick screening. Yes, Michael was color-blind.

I spoke with Michael's mom. I could hear relief in her voice, "That explains why he had so much trouble playing Candyland. We thought he just didn't know his colors. We had been trying to work with him to help him learn them. He just could not see the difference."

I mentioned the results to the school's speech clinician who saw Michael for articulation issues.

"I had Michael screened for color blindness. As it turns out he is color-blind. This could spill over into his sessions with you."

"Did Mitchell get tested too?" Mitchell was Michael's identical twin. She saw Mitchell for speech too. The clinician herself was an identical twin.

"Oh, no, I totally didn't think about Mitchell. He was not even on my radar. He is not my student. It didn't occur to me to suggest that he ought to be tested as well."

"They are identical twins and share the same DNA. Mitchell is likely color-blind too," the speech clinician said, quickly assessing the situation.

Identical twins have the same chromosomes. Their outward appearance and inward makeup are the same.

Image Bearer

Humans have God's DNA. This is the heart of what it means to be human. We are made in His image; He is not created in ours.

Because we are created in the image of our Creator, we are worthy, valuable, loveable, capable, and purposeful. There is hope because the Creator chose to create you and me. He made us and our kids on purpose, in His image, for His glory.

Since we are created in His likeness, we are relational, rational, emotional, volitional, and spiritual. Each one of us carries attributes of God. These qualities set us apart from the rest of creation.

The heavens reflect God's glory, yet they are not made in His image. The rocks may cry out in worship, but He did not breathe life into them. God made the animals; they were good, however they were not made in His likeness. Only humans, daughters of Eve and sons of Adam, are God's children. We are beloved and cherished by God because we resemble Him. Our Father's love for us is enduring, everlasting, and eternal. Even though we have a sin nature, we are worth dying for. We are not perfect, yet we are being perfected. Our sin nature distorts God's image. Yet God continues to mold us to look like Him. We are created to reflect Him.

Relationship Status

We are created for relationship because God is relational within the Trinity. I thought God created people because in some way He needed us. That was wrong thinking. God does not need humans to be complete or to exist. He is self-existent and satisfied within the Trinity.

As relational beings, people have the basic need for companionship, connection, and community. When this need is not met, we feel empty and seek false fillings. When our kiddos have trouble making and keeping friendships or when our young adults have a break-up or divorce, they may look for a quick fix to meet that belonging need.

Hopelessness and false fillings meet when toxic ways of relating occur. Substance abuse, a lack of sexual integrity, sexual sin, promiscuity, or porn addiction are examples of extreme false fillings. Hanging out with others who are involved in a similar sin bent, provides a sense of belonging.

For a time, membership of an ungodly group will satisfy the need for belonging. Members feel accepted, understood. When God stirs discontent in one of the members, it becomes apparent how unstable the relationship is. Common experience is the only reason for the connection. When an alcoholic becomes sober, he loses his drinking buddies. He may feel shunned by them. And perhaps they feel judged by the person changing his behavior. Relationships that were once thought to be solid disappear.

There are other false fillings that are more difficult to identify: people pleasing, jealousy, sibling rivalry, and mask wearing. Hopelessness is sown into these behaviors.

Face the Feelings

God has a mind, emotions, and His own will. God's emotions show His personality. One of the best proofs that God has emotions, in addition to the Bible telling us He does, is that humans, created in His image, have emotions. Jesus, the Son of God, displayed emotion. He is our sympathetic High Priest who understands our feelings.

Scripture has many verses that talk about God demonstrating emotion. Some of the emotions are anger (Proverbs 8:13), compassion (2 Peter 3:9), grief (John 11:35), love (1 John 4:8), hate (Proverbs 6:16–19), jealousy (Exodus 20:5), and joy (Zephaniah 3:17). God is not emotional in the sense of being controlled by His emotions. He does not have mood swings.

Some like to refer to God's anger and Jesus turning over the tables in the temple (John 2:15), to justify their own mad. God's anger, unlike mine, is without sin. It is not malicious, and it is rooted in His holy nature; it is righteous anger. What gets God angry? Sin. He is angered over sin.

Even though God is intimately involved with His creation, His character or will does not change according to circumstances or feelings.

Because our emotions are corrupted by sin, we must exercise caution when it comes to feeling-driven decisions. We may not be able to see life clearly when depression and anxiety take over.

Projecting personal insecurities onto others, stubbornly hanging onto plans, clinging to the past, holding self-limiting beliefs, needing constant validation, and fearing uncertainty get in the way of our human ability to successfully navigate life.

Projecting personal insecurities onto others occurs when a person thinks negatively about himself and assumes others think the same way. It sounds like this, "I know you think I'm _____ (stupid, ugly, forgetful, disorganized)." To change this, reframe your talk, "I believe people think I'm dumb." Once you identify your (false) belief you are ready to work on your own insecurities. Realize your filter may be off and perhaps the response you got had little to do with them thinking you were dumb. Maybe they simply did not like your idea.

Confusion occurs when we stubbornly hang onto plans despite the reality of the situation. "Even though I lost that job, I am still going to buy that new car." This is the inability to deal with reality; stubbornly hanging on when it is time to revise the plan. State the facts and then use the word "reconsider." "I lost my job (fact). I need to reconsider the timing of getting a new car."

Life is static when we cling to the past: "He hurt me. I will never forgive him." Holding onto past pain or regret is a form of attempting to maintain control or dispense punishment. Yet this mindset prevents a person from moving forward.

Self-limiting beliefs sound like, "I can't." "I don't have time." "I'm not good enough." To combat this, adjust your self-talk to, "I choose not to." "I am not able to at this time." "I'm learning how to be better at . . ."

Need for constant validation: If validation does not occur it could sound like this, "No one liked my post. I am going to delete it. Everyone must hate me." The best way to address this issue is to say to yourself, "I am loved by God. Created by God for a purpose. My worth is not based on how much other people affirm me."

Fear of uncertainty: "What if . . ." are the two words that capture the fear of uncertainty. The unknown is scary. One way to beat fear is to say, "Even if . . ." "Even if this occurs, I can still _____."

Sarah's thirteen-year-old son, Hudson, struggles with ADHD, learning disabilities, depression, and anxiety. Sometimes he gets stuck on the fear of uncertainty characterized by, "What if?" Sarah has learned the best way to deal with the *What ifs* is to go there.

"What if that does happen? What is the worst thing that would occur?"

Then together they plan for the *What if*. Hudson knows it will be OK, even if that fear is realized, because he has a plan. He has more control and is more secure when he has a plan for the worst of the worst. His mom tells him, "Going through this makes you brave." She encourages him to do the hard thing and persevere to complete the task at hand.

"Sometimes we need to revisit pushing through. Hudson is learning to deal with some of those fears and he is realizing it is, and he is, OK."

Decisions, Decisions

We are hard-wired to be volitional, to use our own will, make our own decisions, and to live in freedom. Humans love to have choice. Frustration morphs to hopelessness when we are unable to or feel too overwhelmed to make our own decisions.

Have you ever felt like a caged bird? You know the moments when you feel trapped and unable to exercise your free will? I felt like this during the corona quarantine. My guess is many folks felt the same way. I believe that is one reason why (along with many other reasons like the basic need to connect) many people declined mentally during this time.

"If you struggle at all to maintain your mental health, right about now your boat may be taking on water like mine is. On days like today, it helps to remind myself I've made it through 100% of my worst days."[41] —Jodie Utter

Survival mode kicks in when our ability to exercise our free will is stifled. My friend Janelle and I talked about her experience as a prisoner's wife. Her ability to make plans for her family was impacted by her husband's arrest and incarceration. Even though her husband was the one behind bars, she was in jail too.

Janelle says, "I was in survival mode. I could only take things day by day. Having a vision of the future was too much, too overwhelming."

She felt robbed of her reputation, her life, her sons' lives. She feared people would say, "You must have known. You must have approved." She thought she would be accused of being complicit in her husband's crime.

Scripture brought her hope during those five years of her husband's prison sentence. She clung to the promise in Philippians 1:6, "being confident of this, that he who began a good work in you will carry it on to completion until the day of Christ Jesus." God had a plan for her family, for her husband, and for their marriage. Armed with this passage she passed along hope to her three boys. She taught them, God is good, God has a plan, God is on our side. Mother and sons prayed, "God, please help Daddy grow, learn, and get help." She reassured her boys that their father loved them, no matter the poor choices he made."

Janelle did have a choice in her response to people who questioned her decision to stay with her husband during this time. She heard these words many times,

"Why are you still with him?'

"Why don't you leave?"

"He didn't treat you right."

Janelle would recall her verse from Philippians and reply, "I see the work God is doing. I want to be here to see the glory God is going to bring." Hope squeezes under a locked door and shows you where a difference can be made.

Janelle lived in survival mode for many years. She characterized it this way, "Survival mode is when you are simply trying to make it through the current day. There is no future planning here."

Heads Up

Planning involves decision making. Making decisions gives us a feeling of control.

"You never let me decide." "I'm (12, 16, 18, 21)." These statements indicate the need for more freedom and power. Behaviors like running away and rebellion are all indicators of the need for freedom. Allowing your child to have some voice in things that directly impact them provides a sense of hope.

Kids will always want more freedom than we are ready to give. Allow some opportunities to practice wise decision making while they still reside under our roof. The human need for volition is hard-wired into our DNA.

Stinkin' Thinkin'

God thinks. He is logical and rational. We are created in His image (Genesis 1:26) and we have the mind of Christ (1 Corinthians 2:16). We are thinkers too. Like every other characteristic, our sin nature can corrupt a good thing. What things do we think about? What do we feed our minds? Are we guilty of stinkin' thinkin'?

Repetition is one of the most effective ways we learn. Repetition helps us recall song lyrics, memorize Scripture, and study facts. Our bodies are created with muscle memory for skills we practice. Little ones will ask parents to read the same story over and over. Repetition is a teaching tool.

There is a downside to repetition. It can be the vehicle that causes us to perseverate on destructive thoughts and repeat detrimental behavior. We often practice the behavior and the thoughts we would really like to extinguish.

The thoughts we consistently feed our minds with will lead to stronger connections in our brain. Our thought life affects our behavior and belief system. A conscious effort needs to be made to feast on a steady diet of healthy, moral, and positive messages. If we want to believe and behave a particular way, we need to be aware of what we are practicing. The more we think about something the more likely we are to repeat it and believe it.

With hope, Dr. Caroline Leaf in her book, *Switch on Your Brain*, offers these words, "You can get the chaos in your mind under control. . . . If you wired those toxic thoughts in, you can wire them out."[42]

Our brains are more able to deal with our feelings if those feelings have a name. Rather than let emotion float around unchecked, name it, claim it, address it.

We feel anger. What is the anger generated from? Fear? Embarrassment? Injustice? Name the specific anger and put that anger in the proper container. Then the anger is addressed, and stress will be reduced.

Wire out self-shaming thoughts like, "I am so weak." "I am so dumb." "I am so unlovable." Change that stinkin' thinkin' and wire in truth, "Yes I am weak. God is strong." "I don't know everything. God is omniscient." "I feel unlovable. God says I am beloved."

God says we must renew our mind (Romans 12:2), take every thought captive (2 Corinthians 10:5), and use His gifts of power, love, and self-discipline (2 Timothy 1:7) to fight the battle within. We are not alone. God battles with us.

If you or your kids fight depression, anxiety, or fear, you may think:

"I need to get a handle on this." God says, "I am with you (Genesis 28:15), and I will help you (Psalm 118:7)."

"I want to keep my struggle private." God says, "You are not alone (John 16:32). Share your struggle with one another to be encouraged (Hebrews 3:13)."

Use the tools God has given you. Those weapons include speaking with a wise counselor, prayer, meditating on Scripture, and God glorifying self-talk.

Hope Busters
Lack of purpose.
Lack of power.
Lack of worth.

Hope Builders
Practice reframing self-limiting talk, "I choose not to." Instead of "I can't."

Repeat, "I am loved by God. Created by God for a purpose. My worth is not based on how other people feel about me." Replace, "What if . . ." with "Even if . . ."

Hopeful Truths
We are created in God's image.
Jesus has walked in your shoes.
We are worth dying for.

Prayer

Father, there are days I find it hard to believe I am made in Your image. Thank You that You call me Your child. This reminds me I am precious in Your sight. Thank You for loving me, for creating me, and for molding me. Amen.

"There are no *ordinary* people. You have never talked to a mere mortal."[43]

—C. S. Lewis

Chapter 8

MIRROR, MIRROR

So in Christ Jesus you are all children of God through faith.

—Galatians 3:26

Several years ago, I was leading a parenting workshop in St. Paul, Minnesota. One of the participants seemed out of place. She appeared to be at least thirty years older than the other class members.

Lord, why is she in this class? What could I possibly say that would meet her needs? My thoughts settled on the idea that she must be a grandma. Maybe she was here to understand how to grandparent more effectively.

Unconditional love was the topic of one of the sessions. My eyes were drawn to the place where she typically sat. My heart broke for her as I observed tears wet her checks.

At the conclusion of the class she hung around, waiting for others to exit so we could have a private conversation.

"I came to this class because I wanted to know more about God. I am not married and do not have any children. My father was abusive and did not love me." God revealed the mystery of her attendance.

"Your Heavenly Father loves you." God took over and gave me the words she needed.

We cried. We hugged. God brought her to the class so she could hear He loves her. Worthiness began to grow. God stirred hope into her that morning.

Reflection

When looking at ourselves, what do we see in the mirror? We ask, "Who am I?" The answer to this question affects belief, behavior, and self-worth.

"I thought others viewed me the way I was viewing myself. Worthless and with infinite faults."—Kendra

This comment tears me apart. How could she believe this? If our kiddos believe they have no worth, they believe their life is worthless. Our kids need to know we love them. Not because of what they do or what they accomplish. They need love with no strings, regularly expressed and demonstrated.

Even when they misbehave, make a bad choice, step away from faith, they need our love. We love the whole person, with strengths and weaknesses. We love in the good and bad times.

Who I Am

To be fully known and fully loved is an incredible concept. When God invites us to the banquet, we come empty handed. It is not a potluck. We come ready to receive.

I had the great privilege of being the speaker at the Rocky Mountain Friends Women's Retreat in September 2019. The retreat center is tucked away in Woodland Park, Colorado at the Quaker Ridge Camp. The retreat's theme was, Come to the Table.

We talked about how we love to be invited to events. We discussed reasons why we may not RSVP yes. We are not unlike those invited in Matthew 22:1–14. Some declined due to work and others were steeped in sin. Busyness and attitude affect how we respond to the Lord's invitation: anger, bitterness, pride, selfishness, and feelings of unworthiness are qualities that can get in the way of sitting at God's table.

No matter our history, God invites us. Every one of the biblical heroes messed up except Jesus. None of us has skated through life without learning a few lessons along the way. We belong at the King's table because of who God is, not because of who we are. He fully knows us. He beckons us to come and join Him.

As part of the retreat, we read Ephesians 1:1–14 and noted how God views each of us. Check this out. The words Paul wrote are filled with truth, encouragement, and hope. It is hard to believe we are loved so thoroughly and seen with such great love.

"Paul, an apostle of Christ Jesus by the will of God, To God's *holy* people in Ephesus, the *faithful* in Christ Jesus: Grace and peace to you from God our Father and the Lord Jesus Christ. Praise be to the God and Father of our Lord Jesus Christ, who has *blessed* us in the heavenly realms with every spiritual blessing in Christ. For he *chose* us in him before the creation of the world to be *holy and blameless* in his sight. In love he *predestined* us for *adoption* to sonship through Jesus Christ, in accordance with his pleasure and will—to the praise of his glorious grace, which he has freely given us in the One he loves. In him we have *redemption* through his blood, the *forgiveness* of sins, in accordance with the riches of God's grace, that he lavished on us. With all wisdom and understanding, he made known to us the mystery of his will according to his good pleasure, which he purposed in Christ, to be put into effect when the times reach their fulfillment—to bring unity to all things in heaven and on earth under Christ. In him we were also *chosen*, having been predestined according to the plan of him who works out everything in conformity with the purpose of his will, in order that we, who were the first to put our hope in Christ, might be for the praise of his glory. And you also were *included* in Christ when you heard the message of truth, the gospel of your salvation. When you believed, you were *marked in him with a seal*, the promised Holy Spirit, who is a deposit guaranteeing our *inheritance* until the redemption of those who are God's possession—to the praise of his glory" (italics mine).

After reading these verses we picked out the words God uses to describe us, His children: holy, faithful, chosen, blameless, predestined, adopted, redeemed, forgiven, included, marked with a seal, and inherited (family).

We took those words and the person seated next to them, spoke their name with the descriptors: "_____ (Name) you are holy, faithful, etc." God's Word poured over every woman.

The next step the women found to be a bit more challenging and tear inducing. They spoke these adjectives to describe themselves: "I _____ (name) am holy, I am faithful, I am chosen, I am blameless, etc."

This exercise was powerful and hope infusing. When we see how God views us, we gain a different and kinder perspective of ourselves and others.

Another idea, along the same line, is to create an invitation with your child's name and a word that describes how God sees them. "Riley, The King invites you to His table. You are beloved." Except for the letter x, this is an a-z list you can share with your kids.

1. The Apple of God's Eye (Zechariah 2:8)
2. Beloved (Deuteronomy 33:12)
3. Chosen (1 Peter 5:7)
4. Delight (Psalm 147:11)
5. Exalted (Acts 2: 34-35)
6. Family (Psalm 68: 5); Favored (Job 10:12)
7. God's Child (John 1:12)
8. Heir of God (Titus 3:7)
9. Inscribed on His Palms (Isaiah 49:16)
10. Justified (Acts 13:39)
11. Known (2 Timothy 2:19)
12. Loved (John 3:16)
13. Marked (Ephesians 1:13)
14. New Creation (2 Corinthians 5:17)
15. Object of Mercy (Romans 9:23); Overcomer (1 John 5:4-5)
16. Purposeful (Psalm 138:8)
17. Qualified (Colossians 1:12)
18. Rare Jewel (Proverbs 20:15)
19. Soldier (2 Timothy 2:3-4)
20. Treasure (Psalm 83:3)

21. Useful (Isaiah 43:7),
22. Valuable (Luke 12:24)
23. Warrior (2 Corinthians 10:4)
24. Yoked with Jesus (Matthew 11:29)
25. Zealous (Galatians 4:18).

Hope can be built by speaking God's words over our children. Hope expands when we understand how big we are loved. Hope calls us to His table.

Intentional Worth

Believers are not defined by our past, struggles, race, religious denomination, failure, feelings, circumstances, sexuality, political party, or sin. We are who God says we are: His child, chosen, beloved, purposeful, and created in His very image.

My friend Nina has given identity a lot of thought. As she raised her now young adult daughter, Nina was intentional about speaking identity blessings over Jayda.

I learned a lot as she spoke to me about identity and how critical it is. Nina explains, "It is so important, the enemy tries to alter it or get us to question it." She points to Matthew 3:16–17 where the enemy challenges Jesus regarding His identity. This was a total epiphany for me.

Matthew 3:16–17 records this, "As soon as Jesus was baptized, he went up out of the water. At that moment heaven was opened, and he saw the Spirit of God descending like a dove and alighting on him. And a voice from heaven said, 'This is my Son, whom I love; with him I am well pleased.'"

God had spoken Christ's identity. Jesus was His son. Then Jesus was led by the Spirit into the desert to be tempted by the devil. When Jesus was physically weak and hungry following his forty day and night fast the tempter came to Him and questioned Jesus' identity twice and his allegiance once,

"If you are the Son of God, tell these stones to become bread."

Jesus answered, "It is written: 'Man shall not live on bread alone, but on every word that comes from the mouth of God.'"

Then the devil took him to the holy city and had him stand on the highest point of the temple. "If you are the Son of God," he said, "throw yourself down. For it is written:

'He will command his angels concerning you,

and they will lift you up in their hands,

so that you will not strike your foot against a stone.'"

Jesus answered him, "It is also written: 'Do not put the Lord your God to the test.'"

Again, the devil took him to a very high mountain and showed him all the kingdoms of the world and their splendor. "All this I will give you," he said, "if you will bow down and worship me."

Jesus said to him, "Away from me, Satan! For it is written: 'Worship the Lord your God and serve him only.'"

Then the devil left him, and angels came and attended him. (Matthew 4:3–11)

Nina mentioned, "There are people who will attempt to create doubt about our identity." She knows because as a black person and a woman she had voices of discouragement speak to her when she was in college studying to be an engineer.

There are those who pigeonhole someone else based on race or gender. "They tell us who we are not and what we can't be rather than identify our gifts and talents." Nina was determined Jayda would not hear these voices until she was firmly rooted and confident in her identity.

"God chose you to live from the very first minute you took a breath. You are beautiful, compassionate, intelligent, funny, and creative." Nina spoke and prayed these attributes over her daughter.

Nina exposed Jayda to books that contained black history; their home library had books with pictures of people that looked like Jayda. The family chose a church in the same way. Nina and her husband, David, were intentional about building confidence and hope in their daughter.

Our personality and our physicality display the creative genius of God. We are a mixture of His traits combined with our unique strengths and weaknesses.

We seek perfection because we are made in the image of a perfect God. We strive to gain love and acceptance because within the Trinity, the relationships are perfect.

People Pleasing Truth

People pleasing is an imperfect way to satisfy the need for relationship. When we try to please people, our identity is fickle. It is based on the way someone else, other than God, feels, views, or accepts us. Our sin nature causes us to do and feel things that cheapen our identity. Peer pressure and people pleasing are qualities that hang their hat on the feelings and acceptance of others. Ultimately, these relationships never satisfy.

When we see people-pleasing characteristics in our kids, we need to pay close attention. Peer pressure combined with lack of personal boundaries and a diminished sense of self-confidence can lead to hopeless behaviors. No longer is identity based in who God says a person is, now it is solely driven by how other people feel about an individual.

"People pleasing is such a dangerous game; I would run myself ragged and pour out every ounce I had to give and would be left feeling so empty." —Kendra

People pleasing appears selfless and relational, yet it is insecurity. Its goal is to get people to like us for what we can do for them.

Here are a few hope-filled thoughts to discuss with your kids about how to love others well and to be a good friend without people pleasing: It is not your job to make other people happy. It is great to care about others and be cautious. Your job is to love others while you honor God. If you believe your job is to make other people happy, you will never be able to accomplish that. Their happiness is their responsibility. There are those who are never satisfied, they love to complain, are energized by arguments, and enjoy being a victim. You are not responsible for how they react to or treat you. You are only responsible for how you respond to and behave toward them.

I recall trying to get a certain person to be my friend. The harder I tried the more unpleasant she was. No matter what, this gal was not going to like me or even pretend to be nice. Looking back, I ask, "Why would I chase after someone so hard? Is my motivation my difficulty accepting some people don't like me?"

People pleasing is manipulation, not other focused as it appears. People pleasing comes from the need to be loved, affirmed, and to belong. People-pleasing tendencies are not part of being a servant, a helper, or a friend.

If you need to work so hard or pretend to be someone you are not, that relationship is not worth the effort. People pleasing is an attempt to earn love. That type of love is conditional. People pleasing trains others to treat you and their relationship to you with conditions.

True friendships do not require kid gloves. Extend love and grace and hopefully that same love and grace will be extended to you. If not, like me with that one mean gal (as you can see, I am totally over it), move on.

FOMO

The fear of missing out (FOMO) is driven partly by the same need to be loved as people pleasing. The fear of not being a part of a group, is a real thing. This fear has increased due to social media. Pictures and comments about good times litter social media. Those who were not invited to the party know they were not included. Those who fear their life is dull, are now reminded how boring they are.

"Social media feeds into an individual's feelings of insecurity, regret and ambivalence about how they choose to spend their time either socially, professionally or otherwise," psychotherapist Rebecca Ziff says. [44]

Even as an adult I have wondered, "Am spending my time well?" My friend Lucille and her husband appear to travel a ton. I think, "I'd like to do that."

I commented, "Wow, you and John are traveling so much. All the places you have been look so exciting."

"Me? John and me? We don't vacation a lot. I was looking at your feed and thinking the same about you."

We each saw little clips of each other's lives and strung them together. The life we both appeared to be living was not reality.

As we scroll through social media we may feel left out or perceive that our lives are not as cool or robust as someone else's. We are bombarded by highlight reels. Comparison leaves us feeling inadequate. Nothing stokes the fire of discontent more than social media.

"Everybody's life seemed better than mine, in one way or the other. I was constantly comparing myself to others and always finding myself worse off." —Kendra

Comparing usually leads to despairing. FOMO can also create hurt when it is clear we were not involved in a particular event. I know I have felt sad when I was not a part of some gathering.

To reduce FOMO, in *Screens and Teens*, Dr. Kathy Koch suggests that parents implement screen-free days and occasions. She believes,

> To combat self-centeredness that sometimes displays as fear of missing out, we can institute days and places free from digital distractions. This forces us and our kids to truly interact. Our teens need to discover they can live without knowing constantly what's going on with their friends. When the world doesn't end and relationships don't fail when they've been disconnected for a few hours, they realize they may have more freedom that they thought. No one's happiness should be determined by how often they comment on posts or how quickly people text them back.[45]

Here are some ways we can offer hope and assist our kids when they have been a victim of a form of FOMO, the fear of not living a cool life, being left out, or not in the know.

1. First, listen to their heart. Avoid criticizing or offering advice. Allow them to speak so you have a window into their thoughts and feelings.
2. Acknowledge, validate, and normalize the experience of being not included. Share a time (keep it short) when you felt this way.
3. Evaluate the FOMO triggers. Are there certain people or activities that tend to draw up feelings of envy or jealousy? Maybe it's time to unfriend or unfollow certain people.
4. Deactivate accounts or limit social media exposure. Set a time for the family to use social media (include yourself in the process).
5. Create a no phone zone and no phone time. Designate areas and times where phones are not allowed. Protect precious family time and encourage engagement.
6. Practice mindfulness. Be present in the present with the people in your presence.
7. Spend time together. Give your child the opportunity to make some choices in the activity.
8. Make a list of priorities. Evaluate where, when, and with whom to spend time.

Quoting Rebecca Ziff, Margarita Tartakovsky said, "'FOMO stems from feelings of regret, social deprivation and dwelling on what might have been.' . . . This is why gratitude is important. Identifying what we're grateful for and what we do have in our lives helps to 'change our thoughts and feelings away from fear of missing out and toward contentment.'"[46]

Hope Busters
Pretense.
Peer pressure.
People pleasing.

Hope Builders
Read Ephesians 1:1–14 aloud. Insert your child's name into the scripture.
Identify your child's character qualities, gifts, and talents.
Address FOMO.

Hopeful Truths
We are fully loved and fully known by God.
No matter our history, God invites us to His table.
Our uniqueness displays God's creative genius.

Prayer

Father, You have blessed me with personality traits, gifts, and talents. I want to remember who You say I am. Stop the voices of the world from drowning out Yours. Silence the voice of the enemy who says I am worthless because I know I am loved by You. You sing over me with rejoicing. You call me precious, chosen, and beloved. Help me to find my value in who You say I am. I am Your child. Amen.

> Indeed there are those who are last who will be first, and first who will be last.
> —Luke 13:30

Chapter 9

KNOW YOUR ENEMY

Put on the full armor of God, so that you can take your stand against the devil's schemes.
—Ephesians 6:11

Tom, Jake, Jaime, and I drove out to the Family Shooting Center at Cherry Creek State Park. I had never been to a shooting range before.

When I was twelve, I shot my dad's shotgun at a can perched on a stump in the woods. The sound exploded. My arm swung upward in reaction to the gun's force. The can remained stationary. This was not my idea of fun.

Since my daughter-in-love was willing to give shooting a shot, I decided to be a good sport and try it again. I am not a big fan of guns, hunting, or fishing. Not my thing. When I was a kid, I would set caught fish free. This did not make me popular with the fisher-people. However, I knew, by the way the fish swam off, they appreciated my born free way.

We got to the range and put on our protective glasses and shooting earmuffs. Tom and Jake took their turns at the clay pigeons. Jaime and I waited and watched.

Jaime went next and hit a couple. Then it was my turn. My heart was pounding and my hands sweaty.

I shot, missed, and the power from the gun shoved me backwards. This sport was not for me.

The party next to us was made up of a boy of around eight, his dad, and a grandpa. Each one had their own gun.

The little boy noticed the gun I was using was too powerful for me. He offered his. "Hey try mine. That one is too big for you."

How could I turn that offer down?

"Thanks."

After a few instructions from the boy and his grandpa, I took another turn.

I hit two clay pigeons! The boy grinned from ear to ear. My smile matched his. We high-fived. To have success, my weapon needed to fit me.

Get Triggered

Once that trigger is pulled on a shotgun, there is no turning back. The shot is fired, and it may or may not reach its target. That is how anxiety episodes are. The trigger can bring about anxious symptoms unless something happens to block or redirect the shot.

The desire to block anxiety can increase the anxiety symptoms, a self-fulfilling prophecy. The anxious person is caught in the negative self-talk cycle of, "I fear I will have an anxiety attack. I know I'll have one."

Anxiety is worry on steroids. It manifests itself in a physical nature. Shortness of breath, lightheadedness, numbness or tingling in hands, face, and other areas, achy chest muscles, fainting, pounding or racing heart, heart palpitations, dizziness, nausea, sweating, racing thoughts, muscle tension, feelings of losing control, thoughts you might die, or aggressiveness are many diverse symptoms of anxiety. The anxiety-ridden person might be hypervigilant, irritable, or restless.

Once anxiety symptoms kick in, take deep long breaths to stop the rapid and shallow breathing. If you happen to have a paper bag (I know most people do not haul around with paper bags), breathe into the bag. The inhaled CO_2 may reduce the symptoms of anxiety. When breathing in CO_2 you are more able to regulate hyperventilation. The inhaled CO_2 replaces the lost carbon dioxide from the shallow and rapid exhaling. (Note: I did find some research that says this must be done properly and only for an anxiety attack. This may not work for everyone. This is not recommended for someone with asthma, lung, or heart issues.)

If you don't have a paper bag, try these techniques to help in the moment: put your head between your knees, breathe through pursed lip, hold your breath for 10-15 seconds, or inhale through the nose, exhale through the mouth.

Break the Cycle

In addition to breathing techniques, there are other ways to interrupt and break anxiety's hold.

Our kids can learn to utilize coping mechanisms to manage the symptoms. We can teach them to tolerate the triggers rather than protect from the stressors that cause the trigger.

One of our daughters had a fear of loud noises. When we were at Disney World there was a fireworks display. We knew that would be a trigger, so we prepared her. "Courtney, the fireworks will start soon. They are beautiful to look at. They are loud, like an explosion. Get ready. Cover your ears to muffle the sound. Open your eyes so you can see the beautiful colors. It is loud, very pretty, and you will be OK."

Agree with anxiety. "Yes, I do feel anxious. Even though I feel anxious, it is OK. I am safe. God is with me."

Try flooding. Engage in situations that make your child anxious, reassure her she will be OK. Go ahead and take her to the party she feels anxious about attending. Plan to be her support and linger a bit. Let her know you will hang out if it is appropriate or that you will pick her up a bit early. Be sure to do what you say you will do. This is not a crutch; it is a baby step toward conquering fear.

Express realistic expectations. Remind your child he has made it through other difficult situations and things were OK. If your child feels anxious about a test, "Even if you fail the test, you will be OK."

Evaluate the fear. Get out a piece of paper and list the worries. With your child, decide which ones can be controlled. Choose the next best step toward resolving the things that can be controlled and act on it.

Move that body. Exercise to release those endorphins that improve or alter mood.

Turn on the tunes. Put on some praise music, sing and dance.

Make a decision. Check it off the list. Indecision adds to anxiety.

Get grounded. Practice being mindful, present. Notice the sights, sounds, smells, and textures around you. To stay present minded, plant both feet firmly on the ground and take in a deep breath and slowly exhale. Move out of the realm of imagination and move into the present-moment reality, redirect attention to the physical world.

Speak truth. Once you have your mind's attention focused in the here and now it is ready to do some proactive and empowering self-talk.

"I feel afraid, but I am safe. God is my protector."

"I feel unloved, but God loves me. God loves me unconditionally."

"I feel embarrassed, but I can find humor in this. A humble heart pleases the Lord."

"I feel inadequate, but I am capable of dealing with this. God has given me skills to do this. I am capable."

"I feel so sad, but this feeling won't last forever. God says troubles are temporary."

"I feel alone, but God is with me. God will never leave me."

Begin with, "I feel." Then add the statement that is true regarding the circumstance, start with the word, "but". Toss in a spiritual truth at the end. This readjusts the original and imagined concern. Repeat the lines to strengthen the positive and extinguish the negative one.

Stimulate the vagus nerve (located on either side of the voice box) by humming or singing to interrupt the flight, fight, or freeze mode.

Be silly. Humor releases endorphins that combat stress and anxiety.

Tools like humor, breathing techniques, self-talk, agreeing with anxiety, grounding, or flooding may be helpful if used and if success is experienced. Then anxiety becomes more manageable. The anxious person gains confidence in handling related triggering circumstances.

Anxiety's grip is loosened by confronting fears or adjusting thought patterns.

It is a scary thing to have an anxiety attack. Do not hesitate to call 911 if the episode does not quickly resolve.

It is also logical and reasonable to avoid situations that create anxiety. Recovery from a severe anxiety attack takes time. It is totally acceptable not to put yourself or your child into a situation that will create those symptoms. Accepting limitations is a choice. Provide your child with a weapon to fight anxiety, a weapon that uniquely fits them.

House Call

Healing cannot occur without admitting there is a problem. No one would want to admit something is wrong if they are going to be demeaned and ridiculed. Folks who suffer with these conditions need understanding, support, and help. Believers need to be people who can be trusted with another's pain and then assist in healing rather than add to the hurt.

"The word, anxiety, just entered my vocabulary last week."

Ellie continued, "My daughter, Amelia, told me, 'I am anxious, I do not feel like myself. I don't want to feel shame over what I eat. I feel anxious about driving and sleeping. I saw a YouTube video on anxiety. I know I need to see a Christian counselor.'"

Amelia had binged on cupcakes and vegan brownies. While driving she got a flat tire. She was having trouble falling asleep because she worried about falling asleep. Amelia felt like she was not in control. She recognized she has a problem and wants to solve that problem.

"Not getting enough sleep and not eating when hungry are big triggers for Hudson. He will have a total meltdown if those two needs are not met. I'm trying to make him aware of this so he will be able to solve this problem. Right after he eats, the meltdowns disappear." —Sarah

Stuffed Feelings

True statements that identify the feeling, reflect the real situation, and speak of God's promise or character help our kids navigate messy emotions. When feelings are stuffed, they show up at awkward times.

Self-control over my emotions eluded me. I began to weep while on the phone with a photographer in Aitkin, Minnesota. I wanted to hire him for a gathering to celebrate Kendra and Collin's marriage. The coronavirus hijacked their wedding plans. Due to safety regulations and restrictions the wedding we had planned in Pine, Colorado would remain a dream. The reality was many of our invited guests needed to be uninvited.

We decided upon hosting a few smaller get-togethers. One solution we came up with for our Minnesota family and friends was to gather at my mom's cabin on Rabbit Lake in Aitkin, Minnesota.

"The Lake" is a place where many of our family members vacation in the summer. Just two hours northwest of Minneapolis makes the trek up-north doable. The reduced number of people would make the celebration safe.

In the spirit of making each smaller celebration special, we decided to hire a photographer to capture each party. My tearful emotions took me, and most likely the photographer, by surprise. I had difficulty discussing details and making decisions because my brain had become a bowl of emotional spaghetti. My emotions needed to be identified and compartmentalized to effectively deal with the task at hand. Until that moment, I had not realized how deeply I grieved the loss of my daughter's original wedding dream.

No longer were we going to share Kendra and Collin's special day with our extended family and friends. No longer was my daughter going to be able to dance with her cousins and a group of friends at her event. This wedding did not look anything like the one she had dreamed and planned. Covid killed it.

Clear Vision

The awareness of how we feel, along with the ability to name that feeling, gives emotion a home. I pushed my feelings of sadness aside; they pushed back and found a way to sneak out.

When the feelings stop winding around in our brain and find a place to sit, we can work through them. Unless those feelings are identified, exhaustion sets in, indecision continues, poor choices may be made, and tears will be shed at unexpected times.

"Hudson, thirteen years old, is now able to verbalize his feelings because he can identify them. Since he was eight years of age we worked with him to develop an emotional vocabulary. When he gives his feelings a name, I understand him better. His older brother has been a big help with this. The boys talk over Hudson's emotional responses. This has been such a blessing. Hudson used to pick his nails. Now he has stopped. It helps when he describes his emotions." —Sarah

> "I haven't been happy for a while and I don't know why. I just feel angry on the inside for no reason." . . .
>
> We talked and processed a lot of his emotions last week. He took walks outside to calm down. He read quietly in his bed. He yelled just to let it all out. . . .
>
> As [my son] moves into his pre-teen years we are having more conversations about hormone changes and taking thoughts captive and stopping the runaway guilt train over normal emotions, we are also saying I'm sorry and remembering there is grace and forgiveness for our mistakes.[47]

Amber is a tuned-in mom. She is helping her tween son navigate his fluctuating emotions. On Instagram, I commended her for the trust her son has in her and the skills he has developed to identify his emotions.

Amber replied, "We are working a lot on the coping part. It doesn't come naturally to any of us, but in some ways his over expression makes it easier to address vs. one of my other children who simply stuffs everything."[48]

Some people stuff. Others express. But for most, identifying personal emotions does not come easily.

When coaching moms and dads of teens to young adults, we start by doing a check in. We rate our feelings on a scale of 1-10. 1 the worst of the worst, 10 the best of the best. After settling on a number, the client defines the number with feeling words.

This exercise tunes us into our emotions, then we can insert those emotions into the proper container. The spaghetti is untangled, and we are ready to move forward and problem solve. Awareness of our own feelings tenderizes and sensitizes us toward other people's emotions. Our capacity for empathy and compassion expands as our ability to deal with the issue grows.

The Signs

To distinguish worry from anxiety or sadness from depression, we need to know the symptoms. Anxiety has a physical manifestation as opposed to the consuming thoughts of worry. Depression is longer, deeper, and has an air of hopelessness that sadness does not have.

"I would wake up and think, crap, I'm still here." Laura's mom died just before her high school graduation. Laura stuffed her grief.

"To cope I began drinking, drugging, and sleeping around. If I stayed at this college, I knew I would die." After a few failed suicide attempts, Laura left college and found hope. She transferred to another university, came to know the Lord, and found a counselor who validated her and her feelings. She was heard and seen. She felt valued and loved. Her healing had begun.

Here are common signs your child is more than just sad: Lethargy, inability to concentrate, feelings of worthlessness, hopelessness, helplessness, negativity, pessimism, frequent crying episodes, withdrawal, neglecting personal appearance, anger, guilt, unable to make decisions, loss in interest in activities previously enjoyed, eating and sleeping too much or too little are symptoms to watch out for. Depression is more likely to seep in when a person is in their late teen years to mid-twenties.

Reflection Connection

Emotions and our own internal voice can be tamed and retrained. That internal voice is sometimes mean or bossy. That voice is especially intrusive first thing in the morning.

"Almost every single thought that went through my mind was something negative about myself; everything from my looks, to intelligence, to physical abilities. I was a professional at being my absolute worst critic. I found each flaw from inside out and made many up that weren't even true. I conditioned myself to hate all aspects about me. The more I let my mind run on that horrific loop, the harder it became to turn it off." —Kendra

Those first thoughts must be squashed immediately. Talk back to the shaming voice that screams, "You are dumb. You are worthless. You can't do anything. No one loves you."

"On the days I wake up and start to feel those wicked thoughts creep into my mind, that I am not valuable, I have to tell them to stop in their tracks and remind myself that I do have value. It feels awkward telling yourself how great you are but reminding yourself of the good qualities you have and the good things in your life, really does help. (Do this out loud and proud, 'I am kind, I am honest, I have good health, friends, etc.')" —Kendra

Change your cruel self-talk to empowering positive statements. And as Kendra says, "Do this out loud and proud."

Voice your smarts: I am especially gifted in (academics, athletics, the arts, people skills).

Voice your worthiness: I am created in God's image. I am a child of the King.

Voice your capability: God created me on purpose for a purpose. I am capable.

Voice your loveableness: I am so loved, Jesus died for me.

When your child calls out their good qualities, it is a God boast. He gifted your child with natural skills and smarts. Speak those gifts aloud to the face in the mirror to deny the lies the enemy spits out.

Write It Down

In talking with adults who struggle with anxiety or depression, or parents of those who struggle, using a pen and paper aids in understanding seemingly confusing fears. Sarah explains, "Hudson copes with his struggles so much better when he uses a technique his therapist taught him. He has learned to write down three fears and three things he is looking forward to. Prior to the beginning of the school year he was anxious. I asked him to write down his three things he was concerned about. I was surprised to read this, 'I feel worried I won't have the right supplies for school.'"

Sarah was puzzled by this because she checks and double-checks the supply list. Her boys are always fully prepared. She and I unpacked his fear a bit further.

"Could it be more of a security type of fear, rather than a fear of not having the supplies?" I asked.

"Yes, I think so. He and I talked about this a bit more. I realized it wasn't about the supplies at all. He was most afraid of getting into trouble or called out in front of the other kids if he didn't have the *right* things."

Sarah, who also struggles with a mood disorder, would have never known her son was concerned about school supplies and security if she had not had him document his fears. Now she knows how to address his concern and has a window into how he thinks.

Ashley, a mom with social anxiety and depression, has found documenting and assessing her thoughts helps. She processes her emotions and thoughts by using a mood chart. "I assess how I'm feeling: happy, sad, or blah. This gives me the information I need to see if my moods have a pattern. I ask myself three questions, 'What is the trigger? Is there a time of month that is worse? What can I do to change things?'"

Happiness Science

Assessing current feelings by writing them down, helps process emotions. We can also change our habits to increase our body's natural happy hormones of dopamine, serotonin, and endorphins. A person who feels extreme sadness and depression tends to be in short supply of the happy hormones.

"I had soon realized the ungodly amount of energy it had been taking me to start my day, the disdain I felt towards having to go on with my life, to push through the next few hours, as if it were the most terrible circumstance I could have imagined. I thought of my daily ritual of crying myself to sleep, the ever-present lump in my throat and feeling as though I was constantly being suffocated by some invisible outside force. I could not remember the last time I felt 100% happy." — Kendra

Dopamine (pleasure center), oxytocin (the love hormone), serotonin (mood regulator), and endorphin (pain manager) are the happy-type chemicals our brain produces.

To increase dopamine, according to *Psychology Today*, "Eat foods rich in tyrosine including cheese, meats, fish, dairy, soy, seeds, nuts, beans, lentils, among others."[49] To up oxytocin naturally, try these activities: hugging, pet your dog, get a massage, do yoga, give someone a gift, and connect with friends.[50] Serotonin and endorphins are increased with these actions: 10-15 minutes of sunshine each day, eat dark chocolate, laugh, or do a random act of kindness.

Healthy habits, like good sleep, downtime, nutrition, and exercise are personal weapons that can be unsheathed to fight depression and anxiety. A healthy lifestyle sharpens our minds and increases happiness. For good measure, add in hugs and humor.

Hope Busters
Unchecked triggers.
Unnamed emotions.
Unaddressed symptoms.

Hope Builders
Practice mindfulness. Notice sights, sounds, smells, textures.
Practice taking deep slow breaths.
Voice your smarts, worthiness, capabilities, and loveableness to the person in the mirror.

Hopeful Truths
The cycle of anxiety can be broken.
Troubles are temporary.
Sleep, healthy food, and exercise generate happy feelings.

Prayer

Father, You have surrounded me with things that can break the anxiety cycle. Train me to use those weapons of choice in the moments I need them. Give me good sleep, have me crave healthy food, and spur on the desire to exercise. Stop the self-loathing thoughts and replace them with thoughts of how You see me. Amen.

> They have no struggles; their bodies are healthy and strong.
> —Psalm 73:4

Chapter 10

BUILD YOUR ARMY

Do not be far from me, my God; come quickly, God, to help me.

—Psalm 71:12

It was almost six years of waiting before Courtney made me a mom. Tom and I traveled to Bogotá, Colombia to adopt our first baby. Those six years were filled with infertility appointments, disappointments, and adoption delays. Most of my friends were on baby number two before I became a mom.

Tom and I observed friends, family, and strangers, parent. We discussed how we would handle various parenting scenarios. We were more than ready to be mom and dad by the time Courtney was placed in our arms (well mine, I got to hold her first).

I did not want or need anyone's advice or suggestions on being a mom. This was a role I had dreamed of and coveted forever.

Courtney was the perfect baby. As Rosa, from Los Pisingos adoption home, handed Courtney to me, our daughter looked up at both Tom and me with adoring eyes, cooed, and seemed content to be held by us, her parents. Her bottle remained full. She had no interest in eating. Tom and I determined the lack of hunger was due to the excitement of the day.

We brought her back to the Residencia in Bogota. This inn housed international moms and dads adopting in Colombia.

Courtney felt a little clammy. That was understandable; she was dressed in a onesie, white long-sleeved T-shirt, blue dress with dainty white flowers, heavy white tights, and a white button-up sweater. We took her down to her diaper, the onesie, and the dress thinking that would help.

As the evening progressed, we began to realize something was not right. Her diaper smelled yet remained completely dry.

I believed God gave us this child so we should be able to care for her. I feared if something were wrong, we would not be allowed to take her back to the states.

My fearful thoughts and independent thinking got in the way of seeking help. Tom did not feel the fear I felt. He did not believe Courtney's condition was a result of us being novice or bad parents. He realized her issue was physical and the fact was we were novice parents who needed help. He trusted God with the situation by reaching out.

"What would you do if Courtney was your daughter?" he asked Isabel, our Children's Home Society liaison.

"I would take her to my cousin. My cousin is a pediatrician." Concern filled Isabel's eyes. Maybe she felt the same fear I did: What if Courtney would not be allowed out of Colombia?

God had placed Isabel right in front of us, ready and willing to help when asked. I have noticed sometimes helpers are right in our space at the exact right time. All we need to do is remove the fear, pride, or independent streak, trust God, and just ask.

Isabel drove us across the city to her cousin's office. Courtney was severely dehydrated due to a stomach infection. We learned many babies in third world countries die from dehydration. We were not prepared for a sick baby.

The doctor told us how to care for her. If we wanted to keep our baby out of the hospital it was up to us to hydrate her. We made our own version of Pedialyte with the help of the proprietor at the Residencia. Water, carrot juice, and other boiled vegetable water were mixed together. We put the concoction in a large bowl and with an eye dropper squeezed the formula into our baby's dry mouth. We did this for twenty-four hours. After twelve hours we saw tears wet her eyes. Her tears were contagious because we got them too. We achieved success when her previously dry diaper was wet.

My lack of speaking up was composed of pride, independence, and big fear that the embassy doctor would not allow her to travel back to the U.S. Not speaking up could have made a bad situation worse. I praise God Tom had the courage to speak up. God had provided the help; we just needed to trust Him, be brave and reach out.

Our kiddos need to see us seek, ask for, and receive help. Asking for help comes from a place of both humility, courage, and strength. Common sense says no one person can do it all or knows it all. Needing help is not a shameful thing, it is a normal need. We all need assistance from time to time. Asking for help is a hopeful act.

Help Found

God may send help, even if we do not actively pray about it. Our response then is to gratefully accept, receive it, and recognize God's hand in the help.

My young adult daughter Samantha was getting ready to move from her apartment in Los Angeles to Ping Tung, Taiwan. Her furniture needed to be cleared out. She was able to sell a few items. Still a wooden coffee table, a full-length couch, a mirror, and a box spring remained. In L.A. fashion, she moved the coffee table and couch to the sidewalk.

No sooner had she moved these items to the street with the sign "Free" when a pickup truck parked next to the curb. A man hopped out of the truck and began loading the items into the truck bed.

"I have more items inside if you are interested."

"Yes! I have daughters. They need furniture."

He entered her apartment to discover the mirror and box spring, along with a few other items.

"My girls will love this mirror!" Samantha's furniture was a blessing to this man and his family.

He drove off with things he needed, and things Samantha no longer needed.

Even though she had not prayed about what to do with the furniture, God still provided help with her downsizing as He blessed the dad with daughters.

Samantha was being helped while helping another. That is God in the details. She saw His hand at work. She was grateful she could help someone else with the things she no longer needed. I wonder if this dad had prayed about provisions for his girls.

Provision Provider

Trusting God with our needs grows hope. Trusting Him with the smaller things is good practice for the times bigger things show up.

I occasionally visited Samantha when she lived in L.A. On one of our weekends together we planned to go on a waterfall hike near Malibu. We had on our T-shirts, athletic shorts, and tennis shoes. We did not have the obligatory water bottles.

"Should we stop and get water for the hike?"

"No, it's an easy hike, we won't need it."

I did not press it, because surely a California hike wasn't as hard as a Colorado hike. We continued to our destination. I could do without my water.

I really wanted to be cool and sport the same casual attitude about the water as my twenty-some-year-old daughter, but truth be told, my middle-aged body kind of cared about the water.

I said a quick little prayer, "Lord, I'm not going to pursue the water thing. Lord, You know I really love to hike with water. You know my body seems to need it. So, don't let me get thirsty."

The Escondido Falls hike in the Santa Monica Mountains is 3.8 miles round trip. There are a few creek crossings with some rock hopping. It was a sweltering hot southern California day as we made our way to the falls. My mouth was dry. I wished I had spoken up about my need for water. Not wanting to be a whiner, I kept quiet.

Part way through our adventure we came to a steep limestone wall. The tree roots pop out of the side of the hill. They can be used for support. A stretch of rope is also available to make the steep climb of 200 feet to get to the next section of the hike.

"It sure would be great to have some water right about now," dominated my thoughts.

We waited to take our turn to use the rope behind other hikers.

A mom, with a few later elementary-aged kids, noticed me and my lack of a water bottle. Unlike me, she came prepared for her hike. I noticed she had a backpack plus a couple of water bottles. I would have drooled but my mouth was too dry.

"Hey, I have two water bottles. Would you like one of mine?"

"Oh, my goodness. I was just talking with God about this. Yes! Thank you!"

No words, just prayer, and a kind woman brought the needed water before the uphill climb.

Samantha and I exchanged a look and a laugh. God sent a helper armed with extra water.

We Get by with a Little Help from Our Friends

I am so thankful that along the Escondido trail the woman with the water offered hers. I think she would have been OK if I had asked her for some. Although, I would have felt awkward, and I didn't want her to feel uncomfortable. I am thankful God did the nudging instead.

Why do we assume people think the worst of us if we need help? Why do we think they will think less of us when we need assistance? I do not think that way about others; why would I assume others would think like that?

There will come a time, most likely lots of times, when our children will need help. Our kids need to know they do not have to tackle life alone. Not being able to admit help is needed is a western culture problem.

We all need support and encouragement. We are created to be interdependent, not independent. As moms and dads, it is up to us to show our kids asking for and accepting help is a good thing to do. When we feel helpless, hopelessness grows. Needing help is not a character flaw; it is a human condition.

Train your kids to push past fear and that prideful, independent spirit and realize God made us to be interdependent. Dependent on Him and interdependent with others. A confident person asks for help.

The enemy's voice is the one that plays on fears and feelings of inadequacy. "You are a terrible person, parent, child." "If you do this thing, bad things will happen." "People will think poorly of you if you ask for help." The enemy plays keep away; God offers the help.

"The 'vow of silence' I forced myself to take is, in hindsight, one of the reasons my depression got so bad. In my mind, the only thing worse than experiencing the agony of my emotions, was admitting the struggle to the people in my life. I feared the reaction that kind of information would cause. I imagined friends' and family's possible thoughts: disbelief, pity, guilt, embarrassment, disgust, annoyance . . . I couldn't see how expressing this would do anything but worsen the situation, for myself and for others." —Kendra

Hope is found when we seek and ask for help. God even calls Himself our helper. We are created to need God and one another.

"After that night (the attempt) I started telling people one by one what had been going on. I began with my sister and my mom and worked my way to my roommates at the time. It was the scariest, most embarrassing moment, each time I spoke about it . . . but I knew I had to. And to my surprise, each time I was honest and told somebody about what I was going through, I could feel the death grip around my throat loosen just a bit before I started to feel as though I could breathe again. I was now no longer the sole voice of reason (or unreason more like it) in my mind. I had people listening, holding me, encouraging me, and breaking my misconceptions down. And what I had not noticed is how everyone else, prior to these conversations, had portrayed my discontent and struggle. I had come off as stressful and unpleasant to be around. I was exuding the energy I was feeling onto others, which had made them back away even further. It now had made so much sense to me why not many people had reached out to ask what was wrong." —Kendra

Hope can be found when we trust trustworthy people with our struggles.

Hopeful Pursuit

There are times help stares us right in the face. Like Tom's and my experience in Colombia or Samantha's right outside her front door. There are other times we must actively pursue it.

Mary, the mother of Jesus, is a great example of seeking help. Once she understood her calling and condition, she traveled to see and spend time with her relative Elizabeth. Mary embraced hope in a blessed and difficult situation. She was single and pregnant. She carefully chose her helper, someone who would not judge or shame her. She needed someone who would rejoice with her.

Mary chose Elizabeth, a woman who could empathize. In Elizabeth she had a sister in the faith. Elizabeth was "righteous in the sight of God, observing all the Lord's commands and decrees blamelessly" (Luke 1:6). In Luke 1:30, Mary "found favor with God."

Gabriel, a messenger angel, appeared to Elizabeth's husband, Zechariah, and to Mary announcing both pregnancies. Gabriel gave Zechariah and Mary the names of the children. John and Jesus. Both pregnancies were miraculous. One pregnancy to a woman along in age (post-menopausal perhaps) and the other pregnancy to a young virgin.

Elizabeth went into seclusion for five months. In Elizabeth's sixth month, Mary received her visit from Gabriel. Gabriel told Mary about Elizabeth's pregnancy.

Mary could have heard the news and done nothing. Instead she traveled to spend time with her relative who could fully empathize with her experience. In times of challenge we need each other. Just think of the great joy and even relief to be with another person who understood and would not think you are crazy.

Help your kids identify and choose their Elizabeth.

"It is imperative for you to speak to someone about your depression or suicidal thoughts. That being said, use discretion. Not everyone will be helpful, be able to keep confidences, or react kindly . . . be strategic in who you choose to let in. And if you feel no friends, family, teacher, or neighbor will be there for you in the way you need, talk to a professional (that is the next step anyway). Go to a clinic or call your primary care provider and let them in the know. Trust me, they can handle it."—Kendra

Build the Container

Our kids must be discerning when choosing their Elizabeth. Not everyone is a safe person, one with whom to share struggles, suffering, or fears. There are those who will sprinkle judgement or even punishment over a situation. Those folks will use words like woulda, shoulda, coulda. They say, "Well, that's what you get." They ask questions starting with "Why" and "How come . . ." "Why didn't you do things this way?" "How come you did it like that?" "What did you expect would happen?" They heap judgement on an already difficult situation and squelch hope in the process.

1. Safe people listen and wait. They focus on forward thinking and problem solving, not reflective shaming or name calling.
2. Unsafe folks carelessly toss out spiritual practices. "You need to (you should have) pray about that."
3. Safe people say, "That sounds really hard. I will pray for you."
4. Safe people look for ways to help you in your time of trouble. Unsafe people keep you stuck.

We can build a container of trust in our families and in other relationships, as well. As trust is built, hope finds a place to call home. Hope propels us forward. Hopelessness keeps us stagnant.

We want to be our kids' helpers. To be included as safe people, we must remove the "I told you so" shame shawl and "Figure it out for yourself" independent mantle. These words break the trust container wide open.

Loyalty, confidence keeper, wise, discerning, promise keeper, positive, empathetic, prayer warrior, truth teller combined with grace giver are qualities a safe person possesses. They do not judge feelings; instead they ask, "How can I support you?" To be your child's Elizabeth, do not rush to solve their problem or give unsolicited advice. Be a respectful listener. These are qualities I want to possess; ones I look for in others. These characteristics can be developed in our kids and in ourselves.

Here is my list of unsafe qualities: piousness, a shame deliverer, discounter of your story, invalidator, giver of unsolicited advice, problem solver, unreliable, guilt dispenser, weaponizer of private information, gossiper, name caller, and historian.

Examine the two lists. There have been times my name could be found on the unsafe list. I do not have to be that parent; I can choose to be a safe person.

The best safe relationship is a reciprocal, an interdependent one. This type of relationship is one where mutual trust is shared and enjoyed. Offer love and support, and encourage the sufferer to get help. Do your best to keep them safe. When they share their pain, listen, don't judge, avoid criticism, quit asking, "Why?" ("Why do you feel like this?"), rather ask "What" ("What can I do to help?"). Remember you are not the sufferer's doctor or therapist. You are their loved one and support system. It is not your duty to fix them. Be the encouragement bridge to help and resources.

"I cannot express enough gratitude for the friends who never gave up on me and continued to fight for me during this time. I needed people to show me I mattered to them, so even the days I may have been annoyed with their incessant checking in, deep down I was so grateful for how much they pushed me to not give up." —Kendra

Be willing and ready to help them find a counselor or support group. Check back and see how they are doing. Asking the questions does not increase the risk for acting on those thoughts. Asking does not make you responsible if they do act on those thoughts.

Those who suffer from depression or are suicidal are highly sensitive, so be careful with your words. Avoid discounting statements like, "It's not that bad." The chemical imbalance in the brain of those suffering from depression creates a situation where they cannot think straight. They will not be able to react to life events in a way that a healthy person would.

A suicidal person can be a great hider. Others give us a clue into their private thoughts by talking about wanting to die, feeling hopeless, feeling trapped, being a burden, having extreme moods swings, sleeping too much or too little, withdrawing from family, friends, or activities, behaving recklessly, acting agitated or anxious, increased substance use.

"People just don't start acting in extreme and different ways for no reason. There is a means to the madness. If you are noticing someone making drastic and shocking decisions that are out of their norm, there may be a deeper meaning than what is at face value. I urge you to ask the awkward and hard questions, to push through the emotional mud that person is laying down, and simply let someone know you care. In all seriousness, it could save a life." —Kendra

Hope Busters
Pride.
Personal independence.
Private shame.

Hope Builders
Build trust in the relationship by being a promise keeper.
Avoid weaponizing personal information or being a historian of past offenses.
Listen without judging.

Hopeful Truths
God is our helper.
God puts people in our path to be our helper.
We are created to need God and rely on each other.

Prayer

Father, surround my child with safe people with whom they can share their heart. Move them to seek help when they feel fearful or helpless. Use me to be part of my child's support system. Give me eyes to see when they are struggling. Amen.

The LORD God said, "It is not good for the man to be alone. I will make a helper suitable for him."
—Genesis 2:18

Chapter 11

BEHIND ENEMY LINES

The thief comes only to steal and kill and destroy;
I have come that they may have life, and have it
to the full.

—John 10:10

An Alberta Clipper, also known as a blizzard, showed up
in Minnesota in the late night and early hours of January
21-22 in 2005. I flew into Minneapolis from Denver just before
the snow did. I traveled to Minnesota to be with my close and
lifelong friend Maureen. Her dad had his heaven day, and the
celebration of his life was scheduled for January 22 at 11:30
AM.

I was staying with my parents, who also planned on
attending the memorial service. We woke up to over six feet
of snow. I felt discouraged but my dad had a snowblower. We
would be fine.

Every winter season when my dad used the snowblower
for the first time, he would say, "She fired right up. I can always
count on her."

This day was different. She did not fire right up. She did
not even spark.

"OK, Pops, it looks like we have to shovel."

"I don't think so, Lor." My dad had one snow shovel and
one dirt shovel. They were downsizing their outdoor equipment.

"I know God wants me here. I know He wants me to attend
this service. Mom, Dad, we need to pray. I think the enemy is

using this storm to prevent us from going. This is opposition. Let's pray we can get out of here by 11:15."

I marched outside, grabbed the one shovel and started digging. No sooner had I dipped my shovel into the six feet of white when a big snowplow rounded the corner.

I waved him down. "Hey, could you plow the driveway? We are hoping to get to a memorial service in a couple hours."

"Sure."

"How much will it be?"

"One twenty"

Highway robbery! This guy was taking full advantage of the situation. But I certainly was not going to turn down the guy God sent to plow the driveway.

"OK. Thank you."

"Pops, I'll pay. God sent this guy and I'm grateful." I was a bit annoyed that God's person was a rip-off artist.

My dad watched the driver like a hawk, being certain that we would get our money's worth. He even directed the driver to redo some of the plowing. I looked through my wallet and did not have enough.

"Pops, can you lend me twenty dollars? I only have one hundred."

We collected the money.

I handed six twenties through the plow's open window. One hundred and twenty.

"Oh no," he said as he handed me back five of the twenties.

"Only one twenty," God's servant said.

We got plowed out, got a steal of a deal in the process, and made it to the service on time. God takes care of the opposition. Just watch!

Obstacle or Opposition

Discerning whether or not something is opposition from the enemy or an obstacle God has put in place to redirect can be a bit tricky. In Romans 1:8–13, Paul was prevented from going to Rome until God's will and way were opened up to him. God put obstacles in Paul's path until the appointed time.

"I do not want you to be unaware, brothers and sisters, that I planned many times to come to you (but have been prevented from doing so until now) in order that I might have a harvest among you, just as I have had among the other Gentiles" (Romans 1:13).

God uses obstacles to cause us to wait for His timing; the enemy attempts to get in God's way through opposition to God's will.

To determine if God is redirecting the path and plan or if the enemy is trying to mess with the path and plan, state what you know to clarify the situation: God is good. God desires to have all come to Him and not perish. God uses all things to the good for those who love Him.

Faith Shield

The shield of faith, one piece of our spiritual armor listed in Ephesians 6:16, is used to extinguish the enemy's flaming arrows. When I feel fragile, I use this acronym, F.A.I.T.H. , to put out the enemy's weapon of fire and refuel hope.

1. *F*- Face the Day: Before getting out of bed, pray a prayer regarding how you would like to approach the day. "Father, your mercies are new every morning. I feel weak, I receive your strength to face the day."

2. *A*- Awareness of stress triggers in yourself and your kids. Basic needs that are not met (like lack of sleep or hunger) and an inconsistent and unpredictable schedule add stress. Create a routine.

3. *I*- Influences that are negative need to be removed. Choose input that is hopeful and helps you rise to the occasion. Open up and read the book of Psalms where you see God's victory.

4. *T*-Take time to be thankful. Each day journal about three things for which you are thankful. Focus on what is rather than what isn't.

5. *H*-Happiness. Add joy to your day. Get serious about bringing happiness home.

To spur on hopefulness, teach your kids to include these faith ingredients in their daily life. Adversity is a part of life. Offer assistance and assurance. As parents it is up to us to show, equip, and come alongside our kids to help them navigate hard times.

> Now faith is the assurance of things hoped for, the conviction of things not seen.
> —Hebrews 11:1 ESV

Treasure Hunt

Popularity, power, prestige, possessions, and position are hopeless counterfeits. These are the things that can be stolen or destroyed. We chase after them and still never feel satisfied even if we catch a few. We desire more, except the basket has an empty bottom.

"Do not store up for yourselves treasures on earth, where moths and vermin destroy, and where thieves break in and steal. But store up for yourselves treasures in heaven, where moths and vermin do not destroy, and where thieves do not break in and steal. For where your treasure is, there your heart will be also" (Matthew 6: 19–21).

Social media, the achievement culture, adventure junkie, sexuality, relationships, political party, and even happiness are things that can become idols. If we place our hope in any of these things, we are bound to be discontent, envious, and even hopeless. This is what King Solomon called "chasing after the wind" in Ecclesiastes 4:4.

"My son, Mark's, classmate Michael is in constant competition with my boy. He seems to need to prove himself by belittling my son's accomplishments. He says things like, 'I would have made Concert Band too if I had tried out. I just don't have the time because I am taking so many Advanced Placement classes.' I feel sorry for him. He must have a lot of pressure at home to be the best." —Monica

Parental pressure and social media participation keep the counterfeit spin alive. There are many parents who push their children to be the brightest and the best. Add social media to the achievement culture and the result is highly stressed kids.

Young people are constantly and consistently exposed to their peers' adventures, activities, and achievements. While being bombarded with these images, the enemy shouts, "You are not as smart or as happy as they are." He plays on our kids' insecurities. That is a lot to take as a tween, teen, or young adult. And it can be a lot to take as a healthy adult.

Our identity is in Christ. He tells us who we are: beloved, chosen, and precious. We are valuable in His sight. God continues to strengthen and grow us so we will look more like Him and less like . . . us.

Liar, Liar

"He was a murderer from the beginning, not holding to the truth, for there is no truth in him. When he lies, he speaks his native language, for he is a liar and the father of lies," Jesus declared (John 8:44).

God's enemy, the devil, is described as the father of lies. Here are some whoppers he tells those who struggle with anxiety, fear, or depression:

1. Mental illness is not real.
2. Mental illness is caused by unconfessed sin and is a punishment from God.
3. Mental illness separates you from God.
4. Mental illness would go away if you had a stronger faith.

My friend, Melonie, lost her son to suicide. She spoke these words at his memorial service. "I do believe Luke was believing some lies. Sometimes those lies lead to consequences. God has given us the responsibility to be lie detectors and truth inspectors; to discern what is a lie and what is truth. Take those negative thoughts, full of lies, and bring them back to the truth."

Here is the truth:

1. Mental illness is real. It impacts the brain's ability to function.
2. Mental illness, like physical illness, is a part of a fallen world with broken people. Some of the enemy's lies are cloaked in partial truth. It is possible that unconfessed sin can lead to a variety of stress responses. Our soul, when in conflict with the Spirit, experiences spiritual tension. That tension leads to conscience conviction. If you have unconfessed sin, confess it and repent.
3. Mental illness could be unconfessed sin, but more likely it is spurred on by trauma, genetics, or other external experiences.
   "For I am convinced that neither death nor life, neither angels nor demons, neither the present nor the future, nor any powers, neither height nor depth, nor anything else in all creation, will be able to separate us from the love of God that is in Christ Jesus our Lord" (Romans 8:38-39).
4. Mental illness does not separate us from God nor does it disqualify us from serving Him.
   It is a trial God allows (for reasons this side of heaven we don't fully understand). He calls us to partner with Him even in our suffering. Just like He did with Paul and Paul's thorn. "But he said to me, 'My grace is sufficient for you, for my power is made perfect in weakness.' Therefore I will boast all the more gladly about my weaknesses, so that Christ's power may rest on me" (2 Corinthians 12:9).

Here is an additional Scripture to add to your spiritual arsenal:

"As he went along, he saw a man blind from birth. His disciples asked him, 'Rabbi, who sinned, this man or his parents, that he was born blind?' 'Neither this man nor his parents sinned,' said Jesus, 'but this happened so that the works of God might be displayed in him'" (John 9:1–3).

God's plan and purposes are wrapped up in His glory and His will. "I consider that our present sufferings are not worth comparing with the glory that will be revealed in us" (Romans 8:18).

These are verses to memorize to stop the enemy's hissing. God's Word is the sword Jesus used to fight off the enemy. The Word is our weapon too. We must know who our God is, recognize our Shepherd's voice, and recall His promises so we do not sink into the pit of despair.

Plan of Resistance

According to Dr. Caroline Leaf in her book, *Switch on Your Brain*,

> It is with our minds that we reject or believe the lies of the Enemy, the Prince of Lies. It is with our minds that we change the physical reality of the brain to reflect our choices. It is with our minds that we decide to follow God's rules and live in peace despite what is going on around us. It is with our minds that we choose to follow the lies of Satan and spiral into mental, physical, and spiritual disarray.[51]

Tracey Eyster of momlifetoday.com reminds us, "God's in control and He is to be trusted." She goes on to recommend these strategies to parents who wrestle with fear themselves. These strategies could also be applied to children who struggle with any form of mental illness:

1. Recognize how easy it is to let your imagination conjure up false fears.
2. Share your concern with a friend and have her pray for your child for a specific amount of time. [Or as this relates to kids, have your child choose a trusted prayer warrior like a youth leader, parent, or mentor.]
3. Recall specific examples of how God has been faithful to you and to your child in the past.
4. Get involved in an activity that occupies your mind and your energy.

5. Remember that God is bigger than anything that your child is facing. He knows what is going on and He is still in charge.

She concludes with, "Say God's character traits out loud."[52]

God's Promises

Scripture tells us the true battle is not against flesh and blood but against evil. God will never go against His Word. If you know God and what God communicates in Scripture, then you are able to distinguish His will and way.

Hope Busters
Enemy opposition.
Enemy counterfeits.
Enemy lies.

Hope Builders
Speak God's character traits out loud.
Practice identifying fact. "I know this is real and true."
Practice identifying fear. "I know this is my imagination or fear."

Hopeful Truths
Nothing, no, nothing separates us from God's love.
The enemy tries to subvert God's plans.
Adversity is a part of life.

Prayer

Father, help me to recognize Your voice and discern it from the enemy's voice. On the days I feel weak, remind me Your mercies are new every morning. Give me the ability to memorize Your Word so I am ready for battle. Amen.

> Be alert and of sober mind. Your enemy the devil prowls around like a roaring lion looking for someone to devour.
>
> —1 Peter 5:8

Chapter 12

SECRET WEAPON

The prayer of a righteous person is powerful and
effective.

—James 5:16

Tom and I lived in San Diego, California for five years. Our
two youngest children were both born in Southern California.
Because we had no family in S.D. our friends became our
family. We met our new family across the street, next door, at
church, at Tom's work, and even at prenatal classes.

Tom and Melissa, pregnant with their first baby, attended
the same prenatal classes put on by Grossmont Hospital in La
Mesa as we did. We were expecting baby number three.

They were seated across from us, on the floor. They looked
familiar. We hung around after class and discovered we
attended the same church in El Cajon. We formed an immediate
bond which began a lifetime of faith-filled friendship.

Our daughters were both born that July. We had our
fourth and they had their second child two years later.

We moved from San Diego to Minneapolis a year after
our fourth child was born. There are years we are better at
keeping in touch, some years we are not so good at it. The
times we have been able to get together face to face, we pick
right up from where we left off. Friendships like that bless the
soul.

Two moves and ten years later, our son lost one of his
closest friends in a car accident. I called Melissa, "Could you
and Tom pray for Jake? He's devastated God allowed his
friend to die. I'm afraid this will taint Jake's relationship with
the Lord. It's so heartbreaking."

"Of course." When this couple commits to pray, they mean it.

A number of years later I traveled from Colorado to Southern California to present a parenting workshop. I extended my stay a few days so I was able to connect with my San Diego family. One of the evenings, while staying with Tom and Melissa, Tom asked about Jake.

"How's Jake's relationship with the Lord since his friend died?"

"I was really concerned he would be so angry with God that he'd turn away. Praise God, I see no anger or bitterness. I am so thankful."

Tom's eyes welled up with tears. "Ever since you asked us to pray, I have been praying for Jacob. My friend's heart hardened toward the Lord due to a similar experience. I did not want Jake to experience this. I have prayed for him every day for all these years."

Wow. I was blown away. I felt loved, humbled, and convicted all at the same time. I cannot say I would have had the staying power to pray like that, every day for years.

I thank God for my friends. I praise Him for Tom and Melissa's commitment to Him, to their friends, and to prayer. They love well and that love brings hope, hope for a future. God honored those prayers for my son, prayed for by a true friend and a real prayer warrior.

Prayer Partner

Tom persevered in prayer for years. I must admit my prayer life is not as disciplined. My mind tends to wander. I am not his status for sure. I am better able to remain focused when I pray with a prayer partner. Every Tuesday during the school year, for twelve years now, my friend Vicki and I pray together.

Vicki and I pray regarding our ministries and our families. We pray for each other when one of us is too tired, too broken to pray.

My husband, Tom, has been in his men's small group for about twenty years. These guys have deep conversations, study God's Word, and pray for and with each other.

My two sons-in-love, Alex and Collin, both have men's groups they are a part of. These groups will be a huge blessing to them as life continues to unfold.

Commitment and creating a schedule are important elements to keep the community or partnership going. These relationships are not only precious but eternal as well! If you do not have a prayer partner or a small group, I highly encourage you to foster these relationships.

Pray the Scriptures

Some partnerships and groups are meant for the long haul, others are more temporary in nature. This was the case for a four-week summer Bible study I participated in at my church, The Bridge Church at Bear Creek in Lakewood, Colorado. During the month of July, we studied Psalm 145.

As we unpacked this Psalm, we discussed God's character. That led to a conversation about how we had each fallen short of looking like Jesus. We confessed we have failed big-time because we are emotionally depleted, our baskets are empty. We are drained, unable to pour out goodness and grace to our loved ones.

We took another look at that Psalm and talked about the way in which the Lord loves us. We read that passage as if it were a love letter sent only to us. We discovered, for today, we should toss out the idea of being like Jesus and instead receive the love He wants to pour into us. When we began to recognize God as our loving Father and His great love for us, our countenance began to change.

As we read Psalm 145, we replaced the word "all" with our own name or the words me or I. God blessed each of us in this space. His words poured over us like a salve and soothed our weary souls. We left the study feeling full and uplifted because of God's love for each of us.

This practice may be helpful to you and to your kids as well. When your children feel like they have really messed up and are unlovable (or when you feel like that) try speaking the words in Psalm 145: 8–21 out loud while personalizing it.

> The LORD is gracious and compassionate,
>> slow to anger and rich in love.
>
> The LORD is good to [me];
>> he has compassion on [me].
> [I] praise you, LORD;
>> [I] extol you.
> [I will] tell of the glory of your kingdom
>> and speak of your might,
> so that [I remember] your mighty acts
>> and the glorious splendor of your kingdom.
> Your kingdom is an everlasting kingdom,
>> and your dominion endures through all
> generations.
>
> The LORD is trustworthy in all he promises
>> and faithful in all he does.
> The LORD upholds [me when I] fall
>> and lifts [me] up [when I am] bowed down.
> [My] eyes look to you,
>> and you give [me my] food at the proper time.
> You open your hand
>> and satisfy [my] desires.
>
> The LORD is righteous in all his ways
>> and faithful in all he does.
> The LORD is near to [me when I] call on him,
>> to [me when I] call on him in truth.
> He fulfills [my] desires [because I] fear him;
>> he hears [my] cry and saves [me].
> The LORD watches over [me because I] love him,
>> but [my wickedness] he will destroy.

My mouth will speak in praise of the LORD.
Let every creature praise his holy name
for ever and ever.

Praying God's words back to Him is a powerful practice. Praying this Psalm was like getting a shot of spiritual adrenalin. The knowledge of how much God loves us is beyond human comprehension. His love is a love that endures forever. When we know how much we are loved, we are better able to love others and better able to love ourselves too.

Take a Breath

Prayer, during hard times, is a struggle. We want to pray, yet it feels impossible. We ache to hear from the Lord but are at a loss as to how that might happen.

In March 2020 I had the joy of presenting at the Set Apart Conference in St. Paul, Minnesota at the Northwestern College Campus. My workshop focused on prayer. The timing was amazing, God's timing, because shortly after that conference, the shelter-in-place orders were given. I am thankful I was able to present and train the women in the practice of praying a breath prayer prior to the pandemic quarantine.

A breath prayer is also known as a contemplative, listening, or a meditative prayer. It focuses on one word. That word is repeated throughout the prayer. This form of prayer mimics a meditative, centering practice due to the one-word focus and repetition. The purpose of contemplative prayer is to draw close to God and make one better able to hear God's voice by eliminating distraction or noise and reducing anxiety or worry.

As I studied this practice, I discovered it is controversial. Some theologians believe the contemplative practice of repetition with the focus on breathing ushers the individual into an altered state of consciousness, similar to New Age meditation or Eastern religious practices. These scholars warn of deception and express concern that this practice may offer a spiritual experience—one that may not be with the one true God.

Henri Nouwen and others like Rick Warren, Larry Crabb, and Beth Moore would disagree. They believe "being still" is an important spiritual discipline so one is able to draw close and hear God. John Ortberg, author and teaching pastor at Willow Community Church states, "It is one thing to speak to God. It is another thing to listen. When we listen to God, we receive guidance from the Holy Spirit."[53] Focus on the Family maintains, "There is nothing unbiblical or anti-Christian about solitude, silence, and contemplative prayer. Not, at any rate, as they have been practiced within the context of Christian history. As a matter of fact, these disciplines are part of a time-honored tradition. They've been central to the church's spiritual life for centuries."[54]

Then there are some contemplative prayer advocates who believe that humans have divinity within, and it can be reached through contemplative prayer, making the cross of Jesus unnecessary for union with God. This is in effect praying to yourself, as if you are God. This view is not in line with Christian theology.

There are good arguments for and against this type of prayer. I believe the litmus test is the answer to the question, "Does the content of this prayer bring glory to Jesus Christ or to me?"

My sister-in-law, Stacey, prior to becoming a Christ follower, was part of a New Age Religion called Eckankar. She learned how to meditate and do soul travel (her body remained physically in one place while her soul traveled to another).

When she would do this, she told me, "I would feel evil brush up against me."

"Wasn't that enough to get you to stop?"

"No, because I thought I was getting closer to God and that's why that would happen."

Thankfully, prior to mediating she would say the Lord's Prayer. I believe, as she does now, God protected her.

After researching the pros and cons of a breath prayer and considering Stacey's personal experience, it appears when the practice maintains certain guidelines and biblical content it is an effective and powerful personal prayer time for the seasoned believer. Newer believers, those who do not know God's Word or character, may not be spiritually mature enough to use this practice.

For the mature believer, one who knows God's Word and voice, it is a beautiful way to rest and abide in the Lord. We are in a place of listening and receiving. Normally my prayers are consumed with me doing all the talking. A breath prayer is different, it is me listening to Him. I have developed my own version of a breath prayer that includes the contemplative practices with the cautions in place.

I would characterize my version of a breath prayer this way. It is a personal prayer to a personal God that focuses on Jesus and God's glory. It is faith-filled intentionality with a biblical framework.

A personal assessment is needed prior to praying. If your answer is not yes for each of these questions, this prayer is not yet one for you. Deepen and strengthen your relationship before utilizing this method of prayer.

1. Do I know God well?
2. Do I know His word?
3. Do I know His character?
4. Do I know His voice?
5. Am I able to discern what is of God and what is not of God?

God communicates to His people in many ways: His word, the Holy Spirit (John 14:15–31), dreams (Genesis 37), visions (Genesis 15), His voice (Exodus 4), a burning bush (Exodus 3), a talking donkey (Numbers 22), and through His messengers the angels (Luke 1).

Peter, Paul, and John each had personal prayer experiences. Peter's vision described in Acts 10:9–16, Paul recounting being caught up in the 3rd heaven (2 Corinthians 12:2–4), and John's experience which brought us the last book of the Bible (Revelation 1:9).

Perhaps the way we hear from God is less important than the idea He does communicate with us through His Word and other means. Aside from His Word, alternative experiences must be tested against what we know of His character and what is stated in His Word. If the message conflicts with His Word or character, the message is not from God. "Jesus Christ is the same yesterday and today and forever" (Hebrews 13:8 ESV).

Breathe In

If you know God well, are a student of His Word, can discern and recognize His voice and character, then you are ready to learn how to pray a breath prayer.

I have broken down the steps of a breath prayer by using the acronym B.R.E.A.T.H. This prayer is for the mature believer who knows God's voice and His Word.

1. *B*—Be still. Find a quiet and comfortable place to read and to pray, a location free from interruption or distraction. Just as Jesus did when he removed himself from the crowds in order to pray (Mark 1:35). Breathe in.
2. *R*—Remember God's promises and faithfulness. "The LORD God formed a man from the dust of the ground and breathed into his nostrils the breath of life, and the man became a living being" (Genesis 2:7). Breathe in.
3. *E*—Examine your life. Is anything hindering your prayers? Do you need to forgive anyone? Do you need to be forgiven? Ask God to forgive someone who has wronged you. "So I strive always to keep my conscience clear before God and man" (Acts 24:16). Breathe in.
4. *A*—Ask . Ask for forgiveness and ask God to prepare your heart, mind, and soul for the one-word message He has for you. Breathe in.

5. *T*—Thank God for His forgiveness, who He is, and what He will show you.
   Breathe in.
6. *H*—Humble yourself. Be ready to receive what God has for you, knowing who you are in relation to the Lord. "Humble yourselves before the Lord, and he will lift you up" (James 4:10).
   Listen, breathe, repeat.

Wait. Keep your eyes closed, your body still, your mind on Jesus. Wait. You may (or may not) sense a message from the Holy Spirit. This message or word must line up with God's character and His Word or it is not of God.

If you get an impression or a word from the Lord (you may not and that is OK) use your Bible's concordance to look up the word. Close your eyes. Fill your heart, focus your mind, and feed your soul with the scripture that relates to the chosen word, principle, or characteristic.

Choose a verse to read, reflect on, and ponder. Apply what God has shown you. Ask, "How would my actions, attitude, relationship be different if I put this verse or characteristic into practice?"

Often we study Scripture with only our minds and pray without listening to the promptings of the Spirit. When praying, talking, and listening to God, the believer should never empty his mind but maintain mindful focus instead. Meditation in Eastern religious practices encourage emptying of the mind; Christian mediation should not. Be intentional and concentrate on the Lord, His character, and His Word. Be prepared to experience a heart change from the One True God.

Praying this way is a powerful experience. It reduces the typical prayer distraction many of us experience. Concentration is needed to pray like this. A breath prayer is a personal prayer to a personal God that must be done wisely with faith-filled intentionality and a biblical focus.

See to it that no one takes you captive through hollow and deceptive philosophy, which depends on human tradition and the elemental spiritual forces of this world rather than on Christ.

—Colossians 2:8–9

Hope Busters
Prayer distraction.
Prayer discouragement.
Prayer disappointment.

Hope Builders
Open up the book of Psalms and turn a Psalm into a personal prayer. Teach your children this practice.
Find a prayer partner or create a small group.
Train yourself and your child to be still before God to hear His still small voice.

Hopeful Truths
God communicates with us through His Word.
Praying in community is a powerful practice.
God will never be in conflict with His Word.

Prayer

Father, I praise You that You want to communicate with me. Thank You for the gift of prayer. Use me to model prayer for my children. Let them see that prayer isn't only done before meals. Amen.

The LORD has heard my cry for mercy; the LORD accepts my prayer.

—Psalm 6:9

Chapter 13

THE BATTLE PLAN

So do not fear, for I am with you;
   do not be dismayed, for I am your God.
I will strengthen you and help you;
   I will uphold you with my righteous right hand.
                      —Isaiah 41:10

"I knew I was going to fall."

"How?"

Five-year-old Kendra, with her left arm in a purple cast, sat on the bottom step while I tied her shoe. This was an important declaration in the middle of regular life.

"God told me. That's why I didn't cry." And with that, she popped up off the step and skipped off to play outside.

A few weeks earlier, I was seated on a lawn chair at my parents' cabin on Rabbit Lake in Aitkin, Minnesota. My crutches leaned up against the arm of the chair. I saw Kendra attempt to climb and hang from the top of the swing set.

"Oh, this isn't going to end well." I grabbed my crutches to support my badly sprained ankle from a running injury I incurred the previous day. I rose, Kendra dropped. Her arm was in the shape of an S.

I ditched my crutches, got Kendra, and we made our way up the steep hill to our maroon Suburban. Other family members sprang into action. Someone grabbed my crutches; another grabbed a pillow to place Kendra's broken arm upon.

As we were preparing to pull out of the dirt driveway and make a second trip to Aitkin County Hospital Emergency Department, my dad, Pops, poked his head into Kendra's window.

"Pops, this happens to everyone right?"

"That's right, Kenj."

Later Pops told me, "I didn't have the heart to tell her it didn't."

Prep for Hope

Brokenness is a part of life. Broken bones, broken hearts, broken dreams, broken relationships happen. We must have a battle plan that prepares our kids for struggles and suffering. Life is full of happy, sad, scary, and anger-producing moments.

Recognize the times where our kids need resilience plus hope to persevere and gain perspective. To live a hope-filled life we need to expect the unexpected, to be ready for and maybe even embrace the interruptions. The unexpected and the interruptions are the places life is lived.

God could have rescued Kendra from her fall. He also could have provided a soft landing. Instead, He gave her the gift of hearing His voice.

God Dependence

God was with Kendra that day and she knew it. He was her helper as He prepared her for the fall. That word, *helper*, used to make me bristle, as if it indicated a subservient position. I have discovered, helper is a godly quality and helper is how God is sometimes referenced. God calls Himself our helper. He is our ever-present help in times of trouble.

Psalm 118:7 states, "The LORD is with me; he is my helper. I look in triumph on my enemies."

In Deuteronomy, He is referred to as our shield, helper, and glorious sword. God stands with us in life's battles. He is not too big for small problems. Big problems are not too complicated for Him. He cares about all the details of our lives.

Helping differs from rescuing. A rescue is saving someone from a dangerous situation. It requires only one person to act as the rescuer. Helping aids, assists, or comes alongside the person needing the help.

Jesus is the ultimate rescuer. He alone has swooped in and saved us from our sins. Sometimes the Lord will use the technique of miraculously rescuing us in hard times. He also takes on the role of helper. Either way, He wants us to learn to rely on Him, trust His will and way, to be resilient, and hopeful no matter the outcome.

In Chapter 3 of the book of Daniel, we read about three young men who needed to be rescued. Shadrach, Meshach, and Abednego were tossed into a blazing furnace because they would not worship the image of gold King Nebuchadnezzar had made. The king said to the three, "If you do not worship it, you will be thrown immediately into a blazing furnace. Then what god will be able to rescue you from my hand?" (v. 15).

They replied, "We do not need to defend ourselves before you in this matter. If we are thrown into the blazing furnace, the God we serve is able to deliver us from it, and he will deliver us from Your Majesty's hand. But even if he does not, we want you to know, Your Majesty, that we will not serve your gods or worship the image of gold you have set up" (vv. 16–18).

God did rescue them. The three men were unscathed from the fiery furnace. Nebuchadnezzar saw God's power. That was part of the plan.

There are times God does not rescue because rescuing was not part of the bigger plan.

In Jesus' exchange with Pilate in John 19, Jesus points out that God has the ultimate say.

Pilate, frustrated with Jesus' lack of cooperation and conversation, says, "'Do you refuse to speak to me? Don't you realize I have power either to free you or to crucify you?' Jesus answered, 'You would have no power over me if it were not given to you from above'" (vv. 10–11).

God allowed Jesus to hang on the cross to complete His plan for salvation. God's will will be done.

When God does not rescue, we wonder why. Here are some possible reasons:

1. It was not part of the plan, due to a bigger plan or purpose (1 Corinthians 2:9).

2. We lack faith in Him (Hebrews 11:6).
3. It was a natural consequence to sin (2 Samuel 12).
4. A rescue may not be in our best interest (Romans 8:18).
5. God is building our spiritual resume so we can share our story with others (2 Corinthians 1:3–4).

Hope increases when we see things from a heavenly perspective. We ask, "What do I need to learn? How could this help someone else? How might this impact me in the future?"

Capture Those Thoughts

God dependence and a heavenly perspective are two components of His battle plan. Scripture, the double-edged sword, is the offensive weapon that spears negative and destructive thought patterns. There are five daily practices that allow us to break free of those patterns.

Worship. Begin your day with a worshipful heart. List God's characteristics. Document what He has done to shift your focus from what we cannot do to what God can do.

> For you make me glad by your deeds, Lord;
> I sing for joy at what your hands have done.
> How great are your works, Lord,
> how profound your thoughts! (Psalm 92:4–5)

Gratefulness. Make a second list, write down your blessings. A thankful heart brings hope and encouragement. Say a prayer of thanksgiving for God's goodness and gifts. "Every good and perfect gift is from above" (James 1:17).

Reflect. Next reflect on a verse from Scripture. If you are unsure of where to crack open your Bible, try the book of Psalms; it is about in the middle of your Bible in the Old Testament. Psalms is just what the doctor ordered if you are looking for praise, worship, and victory type of verses. Psalm 119:15 says, "I meditate on your precepts and consider your ways."

Journal. Record the thoughts that occupy space in your brain. Pray about each one. Next to your concern write down an attribute of God that can take on this trouble.

Concern: Worry. "God, I'm worried about keeping my job."

Attribute: God is provider. If worries resurface, repeat your prayer.

Break the habit of negative thinking. Eventually those thoughts will lose their power as you repeat this discipline. "Do not be anxious about anything, but in every situation, by prayer and petition, with thanksgiving, present your requests to God. And the peace of God, which transcends all understanding, will guard your hearts and your minds in Christ Jesus" (Philippians 4:6–7).

Post. Choose some favorite and encouraging verses to post around your home. I encouraged my oldest daughter to display her verses on her bathroom mirror and read them aloud as she got ready for the day. Find a spot where you are likely to notice them throughout the day. "Write them on the doorframes of your houses and on your gates" (Deuteronomy 6:9).

Biblical mediation happens with Bible immersion. When we pore over God's Word, we sharpen our sword. Negative thoughts are pierced, and God's Word seeps in, renewing our minds.

Fortitude in Forgiveness

A renewed mind has no space for unforgiveness. Holding a grudge keeps our minds and hearts hostage. When we are stuck in unforgiving quicksand, we cannot move forward. My daughter-in-love has experienced the freedom forgiveness offers.

"My dad left my mom for another woman when my mom was in the hospital giving birth to me. My mom raised me all on her own."

The woman Jaime's dad had an affair with ended up becoming his second wife. With her, he gave Jaime two half-sisters. That marriage struggled as well.

Jaime and her mom had every reason to hold a grudge against Jaime's dad. An affair, drug addiction, and abandonment come to my mind as totally justified reasons why a person would find forgiveness impossible.

When Jaime entered her teens, her dad exited from his second family. He took up residence in his parents' home.

Shortly after his own dad passed away, Jaime said, "My dad predicted he would not live much longer either. He told my grandmother he would die young. A drug overdose took his life."

His mom, grieving her son and her husband's deaths, needed support in planning her son's funeral. Jaime and her dad's sister stepped up to help. His ex-wife and estranged wife chose to not participate in the planning. Jaime at sixteen, the oldest of the three children, helped plan her father's service.

I cannot imagine planning a parent's funeral at the age of sixteen. Learning to drive a car and finally, after two attempts, getting my license was my sixteen-year-old challenge.

My daughter-in-love, Jaime, could have been bitter. She was not. She was better. Her beautiful act of love in planning the funeral of a man who was the cause of much pain was grace and forgiveness in action.

As I prayed about writing this book and the messages parents need to raise hope-filled kids in a hard world, God illuminated this thought: the tools of self-care, resilience, and prayer are not the only ways to facilitate hope.

Grace propels hope forward. Holding a grudge, holds us. There is freedom and fortitude in forgiving those who have hurt us. Forgiveness gives us direct access to hope.

Is that why in the Lord's Prayer, Jesus taught us to pray, "Forgive us our debts (sins), as we also have forgiven our debtors" (Matthew 6:12)? No forgiveness, no hope.

Hope hung on the cross and said, "Father, forgive them, for they do not know what they are doing" (Luke 23:34). True hope was realized three days later. Forgiveness makes hope possible.

Spiritual Strength

A renewed mind combined with a strong Spirit makes us battle ready. John 4:24 tells us, "God is spirit, and his worshipers must worship in the spirit and in truth." God is spirit and because we are created in His image, we have a spiritual component too. We even house God's Spirit in our physical bodies. "Do you not know that your bodies are temples of the Holy Spirit, who is in you, whom you have received from God?" (1 Corinthians 6:19).

God's Spirit and our bodies are intricately linked. I know this analogy simplifies things, but it helps me make sense of how our bodies are a temple of the Holy Spirit. The indwelling of God's Spirit reminds me of a pregnancy.

My daughter-in-love, Jaime, is currently expecting baby number two. (Did I mention I love being a Mimi?) Because her body is the vessel housing this new life, she is careful about what she ingests. Whatever she eats or drinks, her baby does too. She wants to keep her babe safe and healthy. And like most pregnant mamas she will do whatever is necessary to make sure that happens.

Perhaps housing the Holy Spirit is a little like that. We want to honor the fact that God has given us His Spirit. Our soul is our personhood, personality, our essence. The Holy Spirit is a gift from God, indwelling us. That is a pretty impressive honor if you think about it. We are so loved, so worthy that God sends His Spirit to be our counselor and guide.

If we choose things that do not nourish the spirit, if we do not consume spiritual manna like worship, the Word, prayer, and Christian community, it becomes tough to discern God's voice. The enemy's voice gets louder and louder. Our need for worshipping God shifts to worshipping something else: achievement, power, control, possessions, position, politics, sexuality, identity, even happiness. Whatever is your top priority will become the thing you fix your heart, mind, body, and soul on. We are created for worship. If we do not worship our God, we will worship something else.

Soul Food

Whatever has replaced the Lord's rightful place in your heart will not satisfy the soul. Feelings of discontent and agitation will take over. During my years of infertility, my goal of getting pregnant was first and foremost on my mind. I began to spiral downward because I was not able to conceive.

"I can't miss any doctor appointment, ever." I was obsessed with my doctor visits.

"This is my only hope." As those words left my mouth, I was hit squarely with the reality my hope was misplaced.

Tom and I realized something needed to change. We decided to head to Rainy Lake, Minnesota for Easter weekend that year.

Rainy Lake is 360 square miles of pure cold fresh water. It is one of the last lakes to thaw in the country. Thirty-five miles of the lake forms the international border between the U.S. and Canada. Our goal was to seek God in God's Country and discern His plan for our family. A remote get-away was just what the doctor ordered.

We talked, we prayed.

"Lord, show us the way you would have us go."

We decided if the doctor were to suggest a particular treatment, we would stop chasing pregnancy and instead pursue adoption. We had always had a heart for adoption and even had a plan. Have three kids, adopt our last.

We returned from our Easter weekend away, and noticed our answering machine was blinking. (If you can believe it there was no voicemail and we had a home phone.) There was a message from my doctor.

"I was just at this convention. I think we should try this approach next."

The procedure she was suggesting was the very one we decided against.

God was going to give our family new life through the miracle of adoption and my OB was the one to deliver the message—on Easter Sunday! Seriously, what doctor makes a phone call regarding treatment on Easter Sunday? The irony of the call and the message was not lost on us.

To hear God's voice and to follow His direction for our life brings much needed hope in dark times. We cannot recognize His voice if we are not reading His Word.

In Kurt Bubna's book, *Uncommon Hope: The Path to an Epic Life*, Kurt describes the role of the Holy Spirit.

So many people are trying so hard, and they're so exhausted because they've not tapped into the source of God's strength. You and I urgently need the Holy Spirit so we can worship. We need Him so we can do the work of God. We need Him if we are to walk in hope regardless of our struggles. It is the influence of the Holy Spirit that transforms us from the inside out. And without question, to do the supernatural, we need the Holy Spirit who is the giver of God's good and perfect gifts.[55]

Perhaps you agree with Kurt's words. You wonder, how can I tap into God's strength? It is pretty simple. Ask for it in a simple prayer, just as Kurt and I would: "Lord God, daily fill me to overflowing with your Holy Spirit."

Your prayer does not need to ramble on or be filled with fancy Christianese. Keep it simple, just ask. God tells you to ask and He promises to provide. "For everyone who asks receives; the one who seeks finds; and to the one who knocks, the door will be opened" (Luke 11:10).

If you want to increase spiritual nourishment and strength, weave worship, the Word, and prayer into your family life. Let seeking Him and His way become second nature rather than a last resort.

Basic Training

Part of any battle plan includes readiness. We need to know who our enemy is and who God is. "God is good" is one of the truths Elsa Wolff, the director of the fifth- and sixth-grade students at Waterstone Community Church in Littleton teaches her class.

I asked Elsa to share with me the main principles she wants her students to learn during the school year.

1. There is a God. With this she adds, "You are not Him."
2. God loves you.
3. There is an enemy.
4. The enemy hates you.
5. Things are not always as they appear; be careful.
6. You have a choice.

In her conversations with the kids, who God is and who God is not is presented in simple and powerful ways: God isn't a bearded guy up in heaven, sitting on a throne, throwing lightning bolts at people doing bad things—that's Zeus. God does not have a naughty-and-nice list from which He dispenses or withholds gifts—that's Santa Claus. God is truth, grace, justice, and mercy.

The mystery of the Trinity is difficult to wrap our human brain around. Elsa defines the Trinity this way: God is three persons in one. God the Father, He is for you. God the Son, He is with you. God the Spirit, He is in you.

She describes what it means to be a Christ follower: "Following Jesus means having a relationship with Him and obeying Him. God gave us 10 commandments to help us have a good relationship with Him and with each other. Everyone had trouble remembering the ten, so Jesus made it simple. We only have to know two things, love God and love others."

Many of those fifth and sixth graders have begun to discover life is not always easy-peasy. Elsa encourages them to persevere and trust God when the going gets tough by responding in faith.

Elsa, with enthusiasm, has her students, with matching enthusiasm, echo these statements,

"God is good. Life is *hard*."

"Life is *hard*. And God is good!"

God is good, even when life is hard. He is *for* us. He loves us. These truths provide hope in a hard world, for us and for our kids.

God Is Good

God is good, even in loss. Murphy, my rust-colored labradoodle, was the sweetest boy ever. He was my walking and hiking buddy. During some dark times, times in which I felt frozen and hopeless, having my pup to cuddle and care for encouraged and sometimes forced me to get out of bed to feed and walk him. Murphy died at age fifteen. My heart ached.

A few weeks after Murphy's death, Tom asked, "Do you think we should get another dog?" Without our Murphy boy, the house was deathly quiet and way too empty.

Taking a walk without him felt heavy. I could no longer head to Chick-fil-A for a quick lunch because it reminded me of my Wednesdays with *The Smurph*. That was the day we would treat ourselves to nuggets (for Murph) and a spicy chicken deluxe sandwich with lemonade (for me).

I nodded affirmatively. The tears returned.

"If we did get another dog, what would you want to name him?" (Tom had already determined we could get another boy dog.) Since Tom basically named our kids, our agreement is I name the dogs. Of course, we each have veto and input power.

"Toby," I said with confidence. How bizarre, I thought. Why did that name pop out? I've never even considered the name Toby.

In a way it made sense. All four of our previous family dogs had names ending in y: Snoopy, Scruffy, Bailey, and Murphy. Toby fit.

I continued to wonder why I spoke the name Toby. I decided to check out the meaning of the name. Get a load of this! It means, "God is good."

It was settled. Not only did we want a dog, it seemed God wanted one for us, too. And . . . I believe He named our newest dog.

Toby, our apricot goldendoodle, loves to frolic, play with his toys, and have fun. Toby, every time I say his name I declare, "God is good." And Toby, as it turns out, is a Chick-fil-A and hiking fan too.

So Simple

That is it, that is the battle plan. Know the enemy. Know God loves us. Know God is good, He is our helper, and He is with us. He will strengthen us, and sometimes that strengthening comes through suffering. We do not need to be afraid. We have hope because God is trustworthy.

Hope Busters
Personal idols.
Private grudges.
Plans interrupted.

Hope Builders
Pray daily for the Lord to fill you with His Spirit.
Play worship music in the car and in your home.
Post Bible verses around your home.

Hopeful Truths
God is our helper.
The Holy Spirit is the giver of God's good and perfect gifts.
Forgiveness makes hope possible.

Prayer

Father, fill me with your Spirit today. Pierce my (and my child's) negative thought patterns with Your Word. Thank You for the blessings You have given me. You are good all the time. Amen.

Trust in the LORD with all your heart
    and lean not on your own understanding;
in all your ways submit to him,
    and he will make your paths straight.
—Proverbs 3:5–6

CONCLUSION

Onward

Satisfy us in the morning with your unfailing love,
that we may sing for joy and be glad all our days.
—Psalm 90:14

"**M**ake your hopes tangible, manageable, and achievable. Hope that sometime this week you can find a new hiking place you love, that you can find a time for ten minutes today to pray, meditate, and focus on the good in your life, that there's a new workout you can accomplish, or a nice park with a tree you discover to journal under. Small hopes that are fulfilled add up to a boost of joy." —Kendra

Hope for Today

That boost of joy sometimes looks like peace, a quiet content space in my day. I have found that time in my summer morning routine. After Tom leaves for work, I get ready for the day. I shoo Toby off the bed and straighten the comforter and then arrange the pillows. (Did you know, pillows are the adult version of stuffed animals?)

Next the *Tobemyster* and I head downstairs, I grab my waiting cup with milk already added to the bottom of my mug by my considerate man. Tom, prior to leaving for work, makes the coffee. The already perked brew makes my morning. With my steaming mug in hand, Toby and I head out to water the flowers. He romps around and then runs over to me and puts his face in the shower coming out of the hose. He bites the water as it sprays the potted plants.

As I refresh each pot, I take in the view of the open space and foothills beyond our fence. I notice the tall grasses waving in the gentle breeze, feel both the coolness of the shade and the warmth of the rising sun, enjoy the brilliantly colored flowers and their fragrant smell. I hear the birds chirping, watch the tiny hummingbird flit around the purple petunias, and observe the mule deer grazing.

The sights, the sounds, the smells of the morning fill my senses. This routine brings me peace. Kendra suggests when one struggles with sadness or depression to make hopes tangible and achievable. Simple routines that include utilizing your senses help to increase peace and set the tone for the day.

Fresh Hope

As each new dawn breaks, fresh hope is ushered in. My friend, MOMS Together colleague, writer, and Bible teacher, Elizabeth Spencer reminds me that, "God does not give us leftovers."

She is right. He did not give the Israelites leftovers either. He provided fresh manna for them each morning. Manna was a bread-like substance that fell each morning from heaven (Psalm 78:23–25). It tasted like honey (Exodus 16:31). God sent manna to the Israelites as they wandered in the desert for two reasons. Daily, He provided food for His people. He wanted to teach them to trust and obey Him every day. The manna was for their physical well-being and spiritual growth.

God gives other fresh provisions to His people as well: like new mercies (Lamentations 3:23) new compassions (Isaiah 40:31), new attitudes (Ephesians 4:22–24), new heart and a new spirit (Ezekiel 36:26), a new song (Psalm 40:3), and new hope (1 Peter 1:3–4).

Isn't it an encouraging thought that we do not need to operate from a place of depletion? God refuels us with new mercies, strength, and hope for each day. Each day the Lord gives us fresh manna.

Hope for the Future

Nicole is a young mom who suffers from chronic pain. She was hopeful 2020 was going to be her healing year. Yet more pain has consumed the months since January than in most of her years combined.

For over a year, she did protocol after protocol, diet after diet. "There were some periods of relief and hope, also times of loss, grief, and pain. July arrived with more out-of-control, unexplained symptoms. I was desperate," Nicole confessed.

Then she heard a message from her pastor. It was as if he spoke directly to her. His words were balm to Nicole's soul, "Desperation will not be wasted. Desperation will be leverage."

Nicole looked up the definition for leverage: the power to move or influence others.

"So here I am, it's been a long painful journey. I am desperate. I believe God won't waste it. He will use my desperation as a powerful tool to move; to move in me, to move my family. I find it hard to reconcile that I am going to school to become a counselor because at this point in my life, I'm not in any place to counsel anyone. Yet, I have hope, because God whispers, 'It will be worth it.' So, although I have felt things recently that would be hard to admit, I will keep holding onto that still small voice quietly encouraging me, 'It will be worth it.'"

We can move through much if we know God is with us and He has a plan and a purpose for our lives.

Rock Your Story

Proverbs 19:21 declares, "Many are the plans in a person's heart, but it is the LORD's purpose that prevails." This verse from Proverbs serves as a reminder that God is in control. In Kendra's case, her plan to take her life was unsuccessful.

God does not prevent all suicides. I do not claim to know why. I do not understand why God doesn't remove these terrible dark thoughts.

"Reading God's Word can make an incredible impact. However, in my darkest days, the days of wishing my life to end, those words lost their meaning. After years of attempting to pray the depression away, yet seeing no change, I assumed God's promises and love had failed me. I was desperately miserable. There were no phrases read or heard that could have pulled me into the light. I needed to *feel* God's love through those around me."—Kendra

I know of a number of deaths by suicide that have occurred recently: a husband and father in his early forties, a teenage boy, a young man whose girlfriend was expecting a baby, a daughter and mother both ended their lives about a year apart. These incidents are heartbreaking and too common.

Luke, a fourteen-year-old, well-liked, well-loved, hardworking rock climber died by suicide. His parents, Lars and Melonie, are my friends. At Luke's memorial service Melonie tenderly shared these words with Luke's friends, "This is not your fault. None of this is our fault. Pastor Elliot said, 'We all have these questions: What should I have done? What could I have done? But these questions never lead to truth.' We tend to take more responsibility for people than is ours to take. Luke made his choice. We all wish he had not. But it was his choice. Luke would reassure us he is in heaven and he is in the arms of Jesus."

Luke's name means, bringer of light. His mom believes much of Luke's struggle was spiritual in nature. Luke's story sheds light on the serious problem of spiritual oppression and mental illness.

For those who have survived suicide or deal with fear, anxiety, or depression, I implore you to come out of hiding, out of the darkness. The shame of mental illness needs to be and can be erased.

Here are three possible explanations Kendra believes her life was spared.

"Now, either one of three things happened here:

"The sites I found my information on were wrong.

"I have a kick-ass liver and kidneys that somehow managed to filter the poison I had ingested.

"My life was spared for me in a supernatural way.

"And no matter which you choose to believe, or the answer I choose to attribute to my being alive, this moment was a huge turning point for me. Death was now suddenly not an option. The only thing left to do was fight for my happiness." —Kendra

Put on the Gloves

Most people do not want to get dragged into a fight. We wonder, "Can't life just be peaceful?"

As a reluctant student of hardship and heartache, I have begun to comprehend hope is not what society says it is. Cultural hope is false hope built on the wind of good wishes. True hope is the energy that fights for life. Like a palm tree, it stands strong in the storm and anchors our soul in the waves of trouble. Hope rises in the hard and is exposed in the unexpected. Hope is the powerful supernatural offensive weapon to be unsheathed in the battle of suffering. Hope is the quality that takes those dashed dreams in this hard world and replaces them with new vision. New vision helps us repurpose or reimagine our dreams so we can take that next step forward.

"In the end, whether those around you support you or not, you can still deal with this and come out the other side. *You* are the one who has to pick yourself up and decide your life is worth fighting for, because *it is*. Whoever you are, wherever you are at in life, even if you can't see it right now, you are strong, you are valuable, and you are loved." —Kendra

Hope Busters
Deception.
Depletion.
Desperation.

Hope Builders
H-Help. Model and encourage getting help, asking for help, seeking help, receiving help. Have a God dependence and interdependent relationships. We are created for relationship.

O-Out of the box. View life from a heavenly, long-term perspective to get through the short-term hardship, knowing God is good and He is for us.

P-Prayer. Find a prayer partner, learn to pray a BREATH prayer. The prayers of a righteous person are powerful and effective.

E-Expect the Unexpected. We live in a hard world. A world filled with happy, sorrowful, scary, and angering experiences. Raise resilient kids by allowing them to fully feel their emotions as they journey through the hard things with you by their side.

Hopeful Truths
You are strong.
You are valuable.
You are loved.

Final Hopeful Thought

Resiliency is a cog in the wheel of hope. It builds perseverance and strength; necessary qualities to live in a hard world. Resiliency is tenacious. It motivates us to push back against the mountain. Resiliency, the quality that helps us get back up, look forward, and press on. But resiliency is like elasticity—when stretched too much it loses its power.

Hope moves us to get up, look up, and pulls us up. Hope boosts us up to climb the mountain; to go up and over. Hope is supernatural power made up of help from God and others, a heavenly perspective, prayer, preparation, passion, purpose, and forgiveness. We can equip our kids for a hard world by raising them with hope, hope for a future.

I lift up my eyes to the mountains—
    where does my help come from?
My help comes from the LORD,
    the Maker of heaven and earth.
—Psalm 121:1–2

Prayer

Father, give me hope when I feel hopeless. Provide help when I feel helpless. You are my helper and hope-giver. Amen.

For God has not given us a spirit of fear, but of power and of love and of a sound mind.
—2 Timothy 1:7 NKJV

EPILOGUE

Dearest Reader,

You picked up and read this book on messy hope. Maybe you were seeking encouragement and ways to ready your kids as they grow up in a hard world. It is likely you are going through a difficult and even hopeless time. Perhaps feelings of helplessness have overwhelmed you or your child. It is possible someone you love is experiencing depression, anxiety, fear, or worry. I am sorry. I understand your pain. When we talk about hope, we must talk about hard things.

I pray the stories, strategies, and Scripture shared in this book have blessed, encouraged, and equipped you on your messy journey. I hope you feel less alone in your messy life because we all live a life filled with messes.

It has been four years since my daughter tried to take her life. Here is what has happened since that time:

Kendra graduated from college. She became a nurse. Met Collin. Got married. Kendra and Collin have started a ministry called *The Do Good Project*. They will be traveling across the country in Mavis, their RV, to meet, interview, and showcase people who are making a difference in the world on *The Do Good Project Podcast*.

I entered this project with fear. Big fear. The kind of fear that makes one feel nauseous. Every morning, during the writing of this book, I'd awaken with a sick feeling. I was afraid reliving Kendra's hopeless times would stir up those old familiar dark feelings in her. I was scared to revisit the fear of the emotions that would rise up in me.

I held my breath as Kendra told me, "It is hard to go back to those days—."

She continued, "It is hard to remember some of those feelings because I don't feel like that anymore." I exhaled. Thank You, Jesus.

The emotions I feared, I felt. It is OK because I am looking in the rearview mirror. I know where we are now, hope has

169

been realized. We made it through the hardest of times. I am confident God will use all this suffering to help someone else and to tenderize me. Maybe you are the one this book was written for.

Healing takes time. Sometimes those familiar emotions of despair and anxiousness seep back in when you least expect them. Please remember, you are not where you were a year ago or even a week ago. That is success.

With God's help, the tools He has given you, and the people who surround you, you and your kids can live this life.

We do not always thrive. There are days we just survive. Survival is more than OK. Survival . . . survival is victory.

With faith, hope, and love,

Lori

P.S. "Don't be discouraged if your mood ebbs and flows during this 'recovery time.' Even after you start getting help (taking medications, going to therapy, praying, meditating—which I've done all of) you will still have hard days. It is a process and not a 'one moment fix all' type of deal. Give yourself grace and time. For me (at the time of this writing), it's been almost two years since I started working through my issues, and I am still doing so. It has gotten exponentially better, but it still creeps up from time to time. And that's OK."—Kendra

My comfort in my suffering is this: Your promise preserves my life.

—Psalm 119:50

NOTES

[1] FastStats, "Adolescent Health," *Centers for Disease Control and Prevention*, last reviewed March 1, 2021, https://www.cdc.gov/nchs/fastats/adolescent-health.htm.

[2] Dr. Stephanie Thornton, "Anxiety and Depression: The New Normal?," *SecEd*, March 11, 2020, https://www.sec-ed.co.uk/best-practice/anxiety-and-depression-the-new-normal-teenagers-students-schools/.

[3] Pete Henshaw, "One in Eight Students Have a Mental Health Disorder, Official NHS Figures Confirm," *SecEd*, November 28, 2018, https://www.sec-ed.co.uk/news/one-in-eight-students-have-a-mental-health-disorder-official-nhs-figures-confirm/.

[4] Thornton, "Anxiety and Depression."

[5] Dr. Amit Sood, *A Very Happy Brain*, by Global Center for Resiliency and Wellbeing, Stressfree.org, January 12, 2015, YouTube video, 4:23, https://www.youtube.com/watch?time_continue=239&v=GZZ0zpUQhBQ&feature=emb_logo.

[6] Warner Bros. Entertainment, "75th Anniversary, Dorothy Meets The Scarecrow," *The Wizard of Oz*, July 15, 2013, YouTube video 2:26, https://www.youtube.com/watch?v=tCgpLROSNmc.

[7] Emily Scott, "Helping Kids Process Through Tragedy," *Renewed Hope Parenting*, July 23, 2019, https://renewedhopeparenting.com/helping-kids-process-through-tragedy/.

[8] Scott, "Helping Kids Process Through Tragedy."

[9] Scott, "Helping Kids Process Through Tragedy."

[10] Lori Wildenberg, *The Messy Life of Parenting: Powerful and Practical Ways to Strengthen Family Connections* (Birmingham: New Hope Publishers, 2018), 101.

[11] Wildenberg, *Messy Life of Parenting*, 102–3.

[12] Lori Wildenberg, *Messy Journey: How Grace and Truth Offer the Prodigal a Way Home* (Birmingham: New Hope Publishers, 2017), 109–10.

[13] Wildenberg, *Messy Journey*, 110.

[14] Sandy McKeown, interview with the author, August 10, 2020.

[15] "Trailer: *We Are Columbine: Stronger Together*," Channel Z, 2018, video, 1:23, https://wearecolumbinefilm.com/.

[16] Sheila Qualls, "A New View on Race from a Mother's Heart," Speak Up Conference, https://speakupconference.com/a-new-view-on-race-from-a-mothers-heart/.

[17] Qualls, "New View on Race."

[18] Qualls, "New View on Race."

[19] Jason Daugherty, LPC Associate and Kelly Martin, LPC Associate, "Managing Adolescent Anxiety in the New Normal,"(Lecture Notes, On-Line CEU Course, May 29, 2020).

[20] Jodie Utter, phone interview with author, August 21, 2020.

[21] Lori Wildenberg, *The Messy Life of Parenting: Powerful and Practical Ways to Strengthen Family Connections* (Birmingham: New Hope Publishers, 2018), 48–50.

[22] Wildenberg, *Messy Life of Parenting*, 50.

[23] Emily Scott, "Helping our kids deal with the stress of life and the hardships of growing up is an important responsibility we have," Facebook, Renewed Hope Parenting, June 13, 2020, https://www.facebook.com/renewedhopeparenting/posts/2820991278024324.

[24] Kathy Koch, *8 Great Smarts: Discover and Nurture your Child's Intelligences* (Chicago: Moody Publishers, 2016), 16–18.

[25] Koch, *8 Great Smarts*, 19.

[26] Koch, *8 Great Smarts*, 18.

[27] "You Is Kind, You Is Smart, You Is Important," *The Help*, directed by Tate Taylor (Glendale, CA: DreamWorks, 2011), https://www.youtube.com/watch?v=3H50IlsHm3k.

[28] Adele Funk, interview with the author, June 11, 2020.

[29] Kathy Koch, *Screens and Teens: Connecting with Our Kids in a Wireless World* (Chicago: Moody Publishers, 2015), 103.

[30] Carol Langlois, "Teens & the Duck Syndrome," Psych Central, September 19, 2013, https://psychcentral.com/blog/teens-the-duck-syndrome/.

[31] Brené Brown, "Listening to Shame," TedTalk, 14:09, March 16, 2012, https://www.youtube.com/watch?time_continue=869&v=psN1DORYYV0&feature=emb_logo.

[32] Jennifer Vail, "I Have Anxiety and Jesus," Her View From Home, https://herviewfromhome.com/faith-anxiety-and-jesus/.

[33] Vail, "I Have Anxiety and Jesus."

[34] Vail, "I Have Anxiety and Jesus."

[35] Vail, "I Have Anxiety and Jesus."

[36] Vail, "I Have Anxiety and Jesus."

[37] "What Causes Loneliness in Young People?" Healthily, January 31, 2019, https://www.your.md/blog/loneliness.

[38] Michele W. Berger, "Social Media Use Increases Depression and Loneliness," Penn Today, November 9, 2018, https://penntoday.upenn.edu/news/social-media-use-increases-depression-and-loneliness.

[39] Melinda Means, "When my second child was born with cystic fibrosis," Facebook, July 31, 2020, https://www.facebook.com/melinda.means.1/posts/10219359663875128.

[40] Means, "When my second child was born."

[41] Jodie Utter, "If you struggle at all to maintain your mental health," Utter Imperfection, Facebook, August 16, 2020, https://www.facebook.com/utterimperfection/.

[42] Caroline Leaf, *Switch on Your Brain: The Key to Peak Happiness, Thinking, and Health* (Grand Rapids: Baker Books, 2013), 26.

[43] C. S. Lewis, *The Weight of Glory and Other Addresses*, rev ed. (New York: HarperOne, 1980), 46.

[44] Margarita Tartakovsky, "Fear of Missing Out Affecting Your Family? 7 Tips to Help," Psych Central, July 8, 2018, https://pc903.liviant.com/blog/fear-of-missing-out-affecting-your-family-7-tips-to-help/.

[45] Kathy Koch, PhD, *Screens and Teens: Connecting with Our Kids in a Wireless World* (Chicago: Moody Publishers, 2015), 107.

[46] Tartakovsky, "Fear of Missing Out Affecting Your Family?"

[47] Amber Cullum, "As [my son] moves into his pre-teen years," Instagram (graceenoughpodcast_amber),

September 6, 2020, https://www.instagram.com/p/CEy1aG0nJQ3/?igshid=a67q7kzn0ima.

[48] Cullum, "As [my son] moves into his pre-teen years."

[49] *Psychology Today,* "Dopamine," https://www.psychologytoday.com/us/basics/dopamine.

[50] Crystal Raypole, "12 Ways to Boost Oxytocin," Healthline, May 27, 2020, https://www.healthline.com/health/how-to-increase-oxytocin.

[51] Caroline Leaf, *Switch on Your Brain: The Key to Peak Happiness, Thinking, and Health* (Grand Rapids: Baker Books, 2013), 22.

[52] Susan Yates, "Our Kids and Our Worries," Mom Life Today, https://momlifetoday.com/2020/03/our-kids-and-our-worries/.

[53] John Ortberg, The Life You've Always Wanted: Spiritual Disciplines for Ordinary People (Grand Rapids: Zondervan, 2002), 140.

[54] Focus on the Family, "Questions and Concerns About Contemplative Prayer," https://www.focusonthefamily.com/family-qa/questions-and-concerns-about-contemplative-prayer/.

[55] Kurt W. Bubna, *Uncommon Hope: The Path to an Epic Life* (Spokane: Essential Life Press, 2019), 83.